DALIT AND TRIBAL LEADERSHIP IN PANCHAYATS

By the same author

1. Agricultural Modernization and Social Change in India Villages.
2. Dalit Agenda and Grazing Land to Scheduled Castes and Scheduled Tribes.
3. Human Rights and Poverty in India: Theoretical Issues and Empirical Evidences (In 5 Volumes).
4. Primitive Tribal (PVTGs) of Central India: Then and Now.
5. Tribal Development Since Independence.
6. Tribal Education: Implications for Development.
7. आदिवासी ग्रामों में टिकाऊ विकास का यथार्थ
8. आदिवासी विकास: उपलब्धियां एंव चुनौतियाँ (भाग–1)
9. आदिवासी महिलाओं के विरूद्ध अपराध

About the Author

S.N. Chaudhary, a former fellow of A.N. Sinha Institute of Social Science, Patna, Indian Institute of Advanced Study, Shimla and MSH, Paris, is Head, Department of Sociology and Social Work, Barkatullah Univerisity, Bhopal. He has written, edited and translated more than 15 books. He has completed more than 15 research projects, written more than 50 research articles and produced more than 18 Ph. Ds. Dr. Chaudhary is actively associated with many national and international NGOs in different capacitites. Currently, he is working on Technological Modernization in Agriculture and Social Change; Untochability and Poverty among the Tribals; and Gains and Pains of Globalisation.

DALIT AND TRIBAL LEADERSHIP IN PANCHAYATS

S.N. CHAUDHARY
Department of Sociology and Social Work
Barkatullah University, Bhopal

CONCEPT PUBLISHING COMPANY PVT. LTD.
NEW DELHI-110059

ISBN: 978-81-8069-070-9

Edition 2023

Published and Printed by

Concept
Since 1974

Concept Publishing Company Pvt. Ltd.
A/15-16, Commercial Block, Mohan Garden,
New Delhi-110059 (India)
T : 91-11-41101460
E : publishing@conceptpub.com, *W*: www.conceptpub.com

Foreword

In the Indian scenario, social exclusion is not a new phenomenon. History bears witness to exclusion of social groups on the bases of caste, class, gender, and religion. Most notably is the social category of Dalits (Constitutionally categorised as 'Scheduled Caste'). Access to and control over economic and social opportunities have relegated them to the category of "social outsiders".

Today, the social outsider category Dalits --- constitute a sizeable presence of 25 per cent of the total population of the country. Eight states, namely Uttar Pradesh, West Bengal, Bihar, Tamil Nadu, Andhra Pradesh, Madhya Pradesh, Rajasthan and Karnataka account for more than 75 per cent of the total schedule caste population of the country. Out of this sizeable population of Dalits it is interesting to know that only one per cent of the cultivable land are owned by them (while just 15 per cent of the Indian population own and control more than 65 per cent of agricultural land). Access to basic amenities to this group has been negligible.

These concerns were subsequently written into the Constitution of the Indian Republic as Directive Principles, which enjoined the State to promote distribution and control of material resources to subserve the common good and prevent concentration of wealth in the hands few. Articles 14,15,16 and 29 (2) of the Constitution of India seek to protect the weaker sections of the country from discrimination and violence of the powerful segments of the population. Apart from protection, opportunity in the form of Article 46 of the Constitution, that 'shall promote with special care the educational, economic interests of the weaker sections of the people and in particular of the SCs and STs and shall protect them from social injustice and all forms of exploitation'. Central to this directive and other related provisions is reservation, which is used here as a package of Constitutional provisions and their intended follow-up programmes for social advancement of the weaker sections, in particular the Dalits.

In 1993 this policy was extended with the advancement of the 73rd & 74th Constitutional Amendment Acts. These enactments became more important due to the fact that as much as 80 per cent of the total dalit population resides in the rural areas. The objective of this enactment was to involve the social outsiders – dalit leadership into the mainstream of local self-governance. Towards this end 21 per cent seats were reserved for dalit community at all the three-tiers of Panchayats and in municipalities. Out of this 21 per cent one-third seats were further reserved for the women of dalit communities.

Such a legislative mandate has opened the doors of the political arena to the dalit community. Very little has been written on the progress of this new leadership in Panchayats, in terms of their ability to control and access economic and social resources for their own community, decision making power as well as the extent of the Constitutional or legal opportunities being translated at the village level.

As part of a national study, the study conducted by Dr. S.N Chaudhary, Barkatullah University, Bhopal, Madhya Pradesh, on the emerging patterns of Dalit and Tribal leadership comes at an important time, a time wherein to take stock of Panchayat leadership under the Dalits, after a decade of Panchayati Raj Institutions enjoying Constitutional status. The book combines views of not only the new leaders but of community based organizations, government officials and the community members who have closely been associated with them.

This book surely provides an insight into the growing new leadership patterns among the Dalits in Panchayats. This could provide an agenda for civil society actions to strengthen such new leadership and sensitise governance structures in nurturing and encouraging these new leadership to become "social insiders".

New Delhi

Rajesh Tandon
President,
Participatory Research in Asia (PRIA)

Preface

Scheduled Castes and Scheduled Tribes constitute about 16 and 20 per cent of population in Madhya Pradesh. They are unevenly distributed in districts. They are heterogeneous in terms of their social and economic status, cultural heritage and rate of participation in development activities. In spite of similarities between the SCs and STs in terms of their lower economic status over the time the scheduled castes have suffered caste and social structure based discrimination and subjugation but the scheduled tribes have suffered marginalisation primarily because of physical isolation, difficult habitat and ever decreasing status of their nature based support system. Because of backwardness of one type or another both of these groups have suffered in different walks of life.

So far as rate of their interaction with the formal and statutory Panchayat system is concerned, over the time here also due to deprivation and dependence, it remained notional. There are many studies to support the thesis that upto the introduction of the 73rd Constitutional amendment even their physical presence in the PRI was limited and that too through cooption and rarely through direct election. And whether to be coopted or not was determined by the local level dominant social and political order particularly over primordial considerations. Assertiveness on the part of these leaders for the cause of poor dalit and tribal population was impossible. As a result, barring exception the PRI in the real sense of the term did not reach to the doorstep of the downtrodden either from participation or from benefit point of view. There was nothing like devolution of power in the real sense of term. In other words, PRI remain pro-rich and pro-dominants. It did not address the concerns of the poor masses particularly the scheduled castes and the scheduled tribes.

73rd Constitutional amendment is a venture on the part of the state to strengthen the human face of the PRI by making it more vibrant, participatory and sustainable. Critically speaking on the one side 73rd Constitutional amendment refers to the failure of the state to implement the old PRI. By introducing this amendment it has accepted the failure of the PRI in the devolution of power and authority at the micro level. But on the other side this effort also denotes sensitivity and commitment to ensure devolution of power and authority upto the village level. For dalits and *adivasis* there is provision of reservation of seats at all the three levels of Panchayat in each of the district as per the population size of both the groups. As a result of reservation facility today there are thousands of dalit and tribal representatives at all the three levels of panchayat at the national and the state level. Efforts have also been made to strengthen these leaders by the state and civil society bodies. Who are these leaders in terms of their social and economic status? What are their political status and level of awareness? How do they perceive people's problem? What are their experiences in terms of gains and pains in the PRI? How their performance is perceived by "others"? What are their future plans? Do the tribal and dalit leaders are the real response to the problems of the dalits and tribals? Can the plight of dalits and tribals be reduced if not removed under the available dalit and tribal leadership? What should be done to strengthen interface between the marginalized and the PRI? These are some of the broad issues which have been examined in this study.

Many ideas incorporated in this volume have been developed in several of my earlier works and some will find elucidation and elaboration in forthcoming contributions. The book is primarily addressed to the World of scholarship but I have in view a readership of policy makers, planners and thinkers and such other concerned individuals.

I am indebted to many individuals but can acknowledge only a few by name who helped me in the successful completion of the study. I am thankful to PRIA (New Delhi) and its president Dr. Rajesh Tandon who not only sponsored the study on Dalit Leadership in Panchayats, on the basis of which Chapter 3 of this volume is written but he also permitted me to use data and analysis of the study for the present volume. He also kindly wrote Foreword of this volume. I am also obliged to

Dr. Yogesh Kumar, Director, Samarthan (Bhopal) for his cooperation and comments on different parts of the study.

Chapter 4 is based on a study on tribal leaders in panchayat sponsored by the M.P. Council of Science and Technology (Bhopal). I am thankful to the Director General and Principal Secretary, Department of Science and Technology, Government of Madhya Pradesh, Prof. H.P. Garg for his cooperation in the completion of the study. Dr. N.P. Shukla, Dr. Abha Swarup and Dr. Rajendra Dhobal also helped me at different stages of this study. Although formal words of thanks cannot adequately express what I owe to them but my thanks go to all.

Shri Manish Mishra worked as Project Fellow in both the studies. He took pain to stay in the villages of Sehore and Betul for months and interacted with all the concerned. I extend a word of thanks and appreciation to him for the pain which he took and suffered in course of this study.

Last but not the least, I am thankful to all our respondents who interacted with the researcher for hours. I extend similar words of appreciation to all those who directly or indirectly helped us in the successful completion of this study.

May, 2003 **S.N. Chaudhary**

Contents

List of Tables

1

Introduction

Background

Democratic decentralization has remained a basic tenet of national policy ever since India attained independence. Various committees appointed by the Central and the State governments have iterated their faith in Panchayati Raj institution as the most suitable agency for participatory planning to bring administration and development programmes nearer to the people. Such states as UP and Rajasthan had passed Panchayati Raj Acts setting up village Panchayats soon after independence. But the basic thrust to Panchayati Raj was given by the *Balwant Rai Mehta Committee Report* (1957). Actually this committee was appointed in January 1957 to study and report on the community development projects and National extension service with a view to ensure "economy and efficiency". The committee offered two broad directional thrusts. It argued that there should be administrative decentralization for the effective implementation of the development programme and that the decentralized administrative system should be under the control of elected bodies. As the authors of the report would put it, "Development cannot progress without responsibility and power. Community development can be real only when the community understands its problems, realizes its responsibilities, exercises the necessary powers through its chosen representatives and maintains a constant and intelligent vigilance on local administration." Following the acceptance of this report a three-tier structure of Panchayati Raj institution was created in most of the states. But the initial enthusiasm displayed by the state governments for democratic decentralization was soon replaced by apathy. The young plant of Panchayati Raj failed to develop strong roots in most of the states (Singh: 1966). Some of the broad factors contributing to near stagnation if not the failure of the Panchayati Raj institutions were: Lack of proper understanding of the scope and methodology of integrated, multilevel decentralized planning at the district, block and village levels and tasks needed to be performed, restrictions imposed by the government on the panchayats in the performance of their functions, existence of parallel bodies to perform the same functions, lack of technical knowledge and dearth of suitable personnel, inadequate financial resources, politicization of the system, unwillingness to grant authority and power institutions at district, block and village levels, by the politicians and bureaucracy (Randhawa: 1996).

In one of the studies in four villages of Gujarat it was observed that (a) the Panchayats serves the interest of mainly one group, namely, the group of big farmers and rich traders usually belonging to the higher castes, (b) the SC/ST members of the Panchayat are selected by the elite group and they do not really represent the interests of the poor in the panchayat and therefore, (c) the masses of the poor have practically no say in the decision making process in the Panchayat, with the result that the activities of the Panchayat do not serve the interests of the poor in development activities including the special programmes for the poor (Hirway : 1986). More or less similar observation was made in a study conducted in Karnataka. It shows that the village Panchayats are neither fully aware about the functioning of the Panchayats nor they are able to participate in their activities (Gurumurthy: 1987). And the other studies also clearly show that the socio-economic power structure in rural areas does not allow the benefits of PR system to flow down towards the weaker sections.

It is needless to mention that with reference to the marginalised sections, the above state of affair was apprehended by B.R. Ambedkar long back. He was opposed to the introduction of PRI. Speaking at the meeting of Constituent Assembly on the Draft Constitution, he strongly criticized those who romanticize the villages as republics and argued that a village is nothing but be "a sink of localism, a den of ignorance, narrow-mindedness and communalism. I am glad that the Draft

Constitution described the village and adopted the individual as its unit" (Ambedkar: reprint 1995).

But in contrary to this there are studies to prove that because of PRI there is change in the rural power structure in favour of the weaker sections. Singh and Rahim (1989) observed that in West Bengal, A.P., Rajasthan and Gujarat PR leadership pattern and authority structure in rural India have registered a major shift. Gradually, the people belonging to lower socio-economic background have joined the PRI. Similarly Shiviah (1986) said that irrespective of the eharge that dominant sections of the society misutilised the reservation/cooption facility, it cannot be denied that the PRI have made it possible for the weaker sections to get into elective offices and get into the pace of further development. Generally speaking, when elections are introduced in a traditional society, political behaviour and power structure reflect the strengths of the existing base. The author concluded that in West Bengal, for example, the village elite was confined to upper castes, now it is widely diffused. In A.P., for example, there has been a distinct shift away from the traditional land owning type towards a leadership which is economically of a lower middle class weaker section, thanks to the role of PRIs.

Critically speaking in principle, the ideals of Panchayati Raj was based on the spirit of self-reliance, self-help and self-imitation. But in practice different picture emerged. It did not contribute to the formation of effective leadership among cross-section of villagers. The leadership remained in the hands of upper segments of society. It worked for the rich. The masses of the poor did not gain much out of the system, rather they were exploited by the PR leaders.

New Panchayati Raj System

In order to provide new face to the PRI so that it may practically come closer to the common people, the 73rd Constitutional amendment was passed. Actually this Bill was passed by the Government of India in *Lok Sabha* during 1989. It is reported that in *Rajya Sabha* the constitutional amendment could not be carried out in 1989 due to non-cooperation of various political parties. During 1991 the Bill was brought for constitutional amendment in the *Lok Sabha.* Later the Bill was referred to the Joint Committee of the Parliament and it was passed on December 22, 1992 and by the *Rajya Sabha* on December 23, 1992. This Constitutional Amendment Bill was then to be accepted by the states. A number of states assented to it through their legislation within three months of the required period. Out of 29 State Legislatures, 17 passed the constitutional amendment and after getting signature of the President of India and doing required formalities it was made law by a notification on April 24, 1993. After passing this Act on April 14, 1993 and subsequently by most of the states the Act changed into law, popularly it is known as 73rd Constitutional amendment. The 73rd Constitutional amendment has special respect for the concerns of *dalits* and *tribals*. Since the objectives put before the Panchayati Raj in the past were achieved only in the notional sense and social transformation did not continue with fast pace, therefore, society created a demand for the establishment of the new Panchayati Raj which may be highly responsive to social issues and problems. Necessary efforts have been made in this direction, but it is difficult to say upto what extent the new Panchayati Raj system was introduced either due to social demand or due to the vested interest of the governing political party. But it is beyond doubt that the philosophy of new Panchayati Raj system is excellent and futuristic in several ways. Some of the broad features of the new Panchayati Raj system are the following :

(i) There should be a *Gram Sabha* in each village exercising such powers and performing such functions at the village level as the legislature of a state may provide by law.

(ii) Panchayats shall be constituted in every state and in every village and at the intermediate (block) and district levels, thus bringing about uniformity in the Panchayati Raj system.

(iii) While election in respect of all the members of Panchayats to all levels will be direct, the election in respect of the posts of Chairpersons at the intermediate and district levels will be indirect. The mode of election of Chairpersons at the village level has been left to the state government.

(iv) Reservation of seats for the SCs/STs have been provided for in proportion of their population at each level. Not less than one-third of the total membership has been reserved for women and these seats may be allocated by rotation to different constituencies in a panchayat. Similar reservations have been made in respect of chairpersons.

(v) A clear term of five years has been provided for every panchayat unless they are dissolved earlier on specific ground and in accordance with the state legislation. However, elections to the panchayat will have to be completed within a period of six months from the date of its dissolution and before the expiry of their duration in normal course.

(vi) The state legislature have been given the power to authorize the panchayats to levy, collect and appropriate suitable local taxes and also provided power for making grant-in-aid to the panchayat from the consolidated fund of the state.

(vii) In addition, the Finance Commission has to be constituted once in every five years to review the financial position of the panchayats and to make suitable recommendations to the state on the distribution of funds between the state and the local bodies.

(viii) The Central Finance Commission shall also suggest measures necessary to augment the consolidated fund of a state to supplement the resources of the panchayats in the state. Thus, large amount of assured funds will flow to the Panchayati Raj bodies, which in turn will strengthen people's involvement in the planning process.

(ix) Besides provision for finance, the amendment also indicates a set of items in the 11th schedule of the Constitution which may be entrusted to the Panchayats in addition to any other scheme for economic development and social justice which may also be entrusted to them by the state government.

PRI and Social Justice: The Case of SCs and STs

The Scheduled Castes and the Scheduled Tribes have been the victims of social and physical discriminations since long. After independence efforts have been made to extend benefits of development to them not by merely putting them at the receiving end but by making them partner in the development process. In the field of Panchayati Raj also attempt was made in the past to ensure their participation either through cooption or through the direct election. But due to variety of reasons the society did not ensure the effective presence and participation of SC/ST population in the functioning of Panchayat at different levels. The Ashok Mehta Committee (1978) strongly observed that of course there has been practice of cooption/nomination of SC/ST members but they have been used by the dominant factions or their own vested interest. It is a fact that at the village level Panchayat they were found in the less number but at the Block and the District level Panchayat their presence was only notional. Hence, under the new Panchayati Raj scheme special effort was made to increase their number at all the three levels not through cooption as it was done in the past but through the direct election.

In other words, Panchayati Raj Institution has universal coverage in the entire country irrespective of different tiers in existence in various states and Union territories. It is now involved directly (in some) or indirectly in all economic development, rural development and social welfare programmes of the country. Look unfolds itself is a large measure of disparity in the ownership of productive assets as well as in the distribution of income among the various sections of the population. The weaker sections of the country's population have recently become the cause for serious concern among the policy makers and planners. It is felt that the serious imbalances in the matter of assets and income distribution coupled with widespread unemployment and underemployment have worsened the lot of the weaker sections. Hence special programmes and a host of anti-poverty programmes have been introduced to ensure all-round development of every member of society. The planning era in the country started with the initiation and implementation of the First Five Year Plan in 1951. Concern for the weaker sections and the rural areas was built into the planning process from the very start. For instance, quite apart from providing for the amelioration of the Scheduled Castes and Scheduled Tribes, the plan envisaged the establishment of community development project (CDP) for all-round and balanced development of rural areas. The central theme of the CDP was to help people to help themselves. The new approach is to help the target group through identification of vulnerable and weaker sections of society and creation of gainful employment and avenues for such households with financial assistance. And secondly, spatial component plans for vulnerable regions which are entrapped in climatically and geographically different conditions were also initiated. Further, MNP Programme was also introduced.

The Panchayati Raj Institution has multiple role to play. Some would treat it just as an administrative agency; others as an extension of democracy at the grassroots levels and still others as a charter of rural local self-government. What is all the more intriguing is the fact that all these conceptual images would co-exist side by side tending to militate against each other at least in the short-run. None of them could perhaps be seriously pursued. This has led to crisis of expectations all along the line.

The Constitution has envisaged as mentioned earlier a crucial role for the state in the protection and promotion of the educational and economic interests of the weaker sections. The article 46 of the Constitution states "The states shall promote with special care educational and economic interests of the weaker sections of the people and in particular of the Scheduled Castes and Scheduled Tribes and shall protect them from social injustice and all forms of exploitation." Apart from these, the Directive Principles of state policy as also numerous other constitutional provisions and statutes enjoin to protect the interests of the weaker sections. Ashok Mehta Committee (1978) documents the inability of Panchayati Raj Institutions to promote the interest of the weaker sections. The Bengirwar Committee on Panchayati Raj in Maharashtra observed "The efforts at the organisational level of the Panchayati Raj bodies or at the individual level of the Office bearers was grievously lacking in zeal and content." It has been alleged that intimidation, coercion and exercise of undue influence have been used by the powerful and economically better off sections to prevent the weaker sections from effectively participating in the electoral process. The system of cooption/nomination of scheduled castes/scheduled tribes has also been so manipulated that the nominated/coopted members are generally allied to the dominant factions. Further, representation of scheduled castes/scheduled tribes is not proportionate to their population since the Acts specify the reservation by a particular number uniformly.

In some states, despite, reservation of seats for tribals in Panchayati Raj bodies, important standing committee have been captured by non-tribals. The funds provided for weaker sections have been inadequate. Population of scheduled castes/scheduled tribes is also not taken into account for fixing the quantum of funds. In one district where tribals account for 40 per cent of the population, the Zilla Parishad reportedly spent less than 1 per cent on the tribals. Further, another study has revealed that funds reserved for welfare of the backward classes in state were much below the prescribed percentage. Similarly, funds earmarked for welfare of weaker sections are, more often then not, either diverted to other sectors or not utilized to the desired extent. For example, in one state 22 per cent of Zilla Parishads spent only about 1 per cent on the weaker areas.

On this factual information the following comments may be made: that the Panchayati Raj Institutions are often dominated by the privileged classes which are averse to paying any sympa-thetic attention to weaker sections; and the PRIs are structurally incompetent to execute effectively schemes designed for the target group and hence many shortfalls occur. Both these criticisms have to be carefully looked into in order to provide for protective or remedial measures and promote constructive action, which is a categorical imperative in view of the fact that over one-fifth of India's population comprises of the scheduled castes and scheduled tribes. Scheduled castes, on account of certain traditional disabilities, and the scheduled tribes mainly because of their geographical isolation, have been disadvantaged and have failed to derive, in an adequate measure, the benefits of planning and economic development of the country. The problem is also aggravated due to their dependence on land and a particular occupational pattern. The bulk of the rural poor are again, largely dependent on land based occupations for their economy. The number of landless labourers among the SC and ST is more as compared to other sections.

It is worthwhile to mention that in the State Acts provision for reservation of seats for SC, ST and women are mandatory. The PR Acts in several states provide for statutory representations for SC and ST members in proportion to their share in the population. A desirable feature of the Karnataka Act is the prescription of a minimum of 15 per cent seats for SC and 3 per cent seats for ST. Further all the state Acts have provided for the mandatory one-third seats for women in each category. All these states have also made reservation for backward castes, though it is a non-mandatory provision.

It is because of the reservation facility alone that at all the three levels of the PRI there are large number of *Dalit* and *Tribal* representatives which was practically impossible before the 73rd Constitutional amendment. The following Table 1.1 shows the scenario at the village level in different parts of the country.

Table 1.1 : Category of Members of PRI (at village level) in selected states

State	Total No. of members (elected/coopted/nominated)	SC/ST Members	Percentage of SC/ST Population	
			SC	ST
A.P	187288	33303(17.8%)	14.87	5.93
Bihar	104877	23303(22.2%)	14.51	8.31
Gujarat	120263	29422(24.5%)	7.15	14.22
Haryana	35450	7791(22.0%)	19.07	—
Kerala	10204	1001(9.8%)	10.02	1.03
M.P.	232989	102222(43.8%)	14.10	22.97
Maharashtra	220595	11244(5.0%)	7.14	9.19
Manipur	1079	39(3.6%)	1.25	27.30
Orissa	67117	28952(43.1%)	14.66	22.43
Punjab	90098	14061(15.6%)	26.87	—
Sikkim	829	286(34.5%)	5.78	23.27
Tamil Nadu	146357	8858(6.0%)	18.35	1.07
Total	1217146	260485(21.4%)		

Source : Rao, Y. Bhaskar (2001): *Emerging Leadership among SCs and STs under New Panchayati Raj Act in Karnataka*, Hyderabad: NIRD.

Hence, today it is a fact that thousands of Panchayat Representatives, both at the national and state level, are from the marginalised section. Moreover, majority of them have occupied this position mainly due to reservation facility. Therefore, they have obtained the first and the most important position responsible for their participation in PRI activities especially for the development of the marginalised sections of society.

PRI and Dalit and Tribal leadership in M.P.

In order to ensure participation of dalits and tribals at all the three levels of panchayat not only effort was made to reserve seats in different districts in M.P. depending upon their population size, but also efforts were made to empower them through different means. As a result of the reservation facility at all the three levels currently there are 52726 SC members, i.e. almost 16 per cent of the total (329788) panchayat representatives. This percentage is similar at all the three levels. For example, out of 45 ZP Presidents 7, of 729 ZP members 114, of 312 JP Presidents 40, of 6399 JP Members 1025, of 21721 Sarpanches 3172 and of 300582 GP Members 48368 are the members from scheduled castes. This is clear from Table 1.2.

Table 1.2 : Classification of Panchayat Representatives in M.P. on the basis of Caste/Community[1] (1999)

Level	SC		ST		OBC		Unreserved		Total	
	Fre.	%	Fre.	%	Fre.	%	Fre.	%	Fre.	%
ZP Presidents	7	16	8	18	17	37	13	29	45	100
ZP Members	114	16	186	25	211	29	218	30	729	100
JP Presidents	40	13	115	36	80	26	77	25	312	100
JP Members	1025	16	1712	27	1706	26	1956	31	6399	100
GP Presidents	3172	15	7299	33	5222	24	6028	28	21721	100
GP Members	48368	16	81541	27	71793	24	98880	33	300582	100
Total	52726	16	90861	28	79029	24	107172	32	329788	100
Population size in per cent[2]	–	14.05	–	26.62	–	42.55	–	12.88	4.80 (minority)	100

Source : 1. Information obtained from the office of the Director, Panchayat and Rural Development Deptt., Govt. of M.P., Bhopal dated 22-11-2002.
2. Census Report, 1931.

As stated earlier, besides the reservation facility which led to joining of thousands of dalits and tribals in the PRI various efforts like training programme for panchayat representatives, provision of no confidence motion on objective basis, as well as intervention of NGO have been ensured for the empowerment of panchayat leaders particularly with reference to the dalit representatives. Also, during last few years many provisions have been made to safeguard dalit representatives from any type of encroachment. However, the socio-economic environment in the villages are still particularistic and not necessarily in favour of the dalit's empowerment. In fact there is conflict between democratic values and socio-cultural values. In such a situation how and to what extent dalit leaders in Panchayati Raj feel empowered and active from the point of view of development of common dalit under their leadership is a matter of investigation. The present study is a venture in this regard. More specifically the purpose of this study is to comprehend the experiences of dalit and tribal leaders in panchayat, their success and future strategies from the point of view of their own empowerment as well as the empowerment of the common dalits and tribals under the banner of their leadership.

Organization of the Book

The book is divided into five chapters. Opening chapter deals with the history of Panchayat Raj institution and the place of Scheduled Caste and Scheduled Tribe leadership. It deals with the status of SC and ST leadership in Panchayat after the introduction of the 73rd Constitutional amendment. Chapter second explains the gist of some of the studies conducted in different parts of the country on interface between Panchayat and the SC and ST leaderships and its socio-economic and political implications. Chapter third is divided into six sections. While section one mentioned the methodological aspects, the second part is an exploration of socio-economic profile of the dalit leadership in panchayat in the study area of Sehore district. Section third is an attempt to map the level of awareness of the respondents, particularly the representatives. Section four deals with achievement and expectation of Panchayat representatives as comprehended by them. Further, we have comprehended the perception of others, viz. community members, government officials and the local NGOs regarding the overall functioning and non-functioning of PRI under the emerging dalit leadership. Towards the end case studies have been presented to examine the success and failure of Dalit leadership. Chapter four is also divided into six sections. In this case also the opening section deals with methodology used in the study. In this study also the main instrument of data collection was the interview schedule. 250 PRI representatives had participated in the study. Section second deals with social and economic profile of these representatives. Section third deals with the level and sources of awareness of these representatives. Section four analyses the level of achievement and expectation of these representatives. Further section five deals with the perception of "others" about the functioning of PRI under the tribal leadership. Towards the end some case studies of selected tribal respondents have been presented.

The last chapter deals with summary of the study. Also, an attempt has been made to suggest steps in order to ensure and strengthen interface between Panchayat and the dalit/tribal leadership.

2

Review of Literature

Trends of studies/research on the Panchayati Raj institution is an old phenomena. However, majority of these studies concentrate on the examination of relationship between panchayats and others sister institutions at different levels, functioning of Panchayat, reasons of its success and failure and so on. The issue of rural development, decentralization of political power among different social groups, constraints and the implications of PRI from the point of view of social transformation got prominence in these studies. However, the theme of interrelationship between PRI and the tribals and dalits did not get prominence in research. This was perhaps because (a) dalits and tribals were seldom involved in the statutory Panchayat institution in the meaningful fashion as many of them are today, (b) their presence was almost notional at the macro level politics, they were really not perceived as significant political entity till date since independence, and (c) they were not perceived as an effective instrument of social change and development. However, the new PRI under the 73rd Constitutional amendment, is a radical departure from the earlier system in the sense that now reservation facility is made available to them at all the three levels of the PRI as per the percentage of their numerical strength. As a result, tribal and dalit representatives are found in large number at all the levels. They are from different social and demographic background. Some are illiterate, aged and poor and the others are rich, educated and influentials. Their level of education is generally low. However, in spite of similarity, reasons of their entry in the Panchayat politics, style of functioning, achievements and the process of empowerment may be different due to different cultural context. Some tribal representatives have attained commendable job, the others could not? They have different experience and perceptions. Why this variation? In order to search answer to these questions various studies have been conducted.

The present chapter neither review a large number of studies conducted on interface between Panchayat and dalits and tribals nor it attempts to review the related literature from all the states where the new PRI was introduced. In fact the review intends to trace a general trends which has emerged among them due to reservation facility in the PRI. More specifically, this chapter attempts to review some of the related publications in the light of the following broad issues.

Who are these representatives in terms of their background? How and why they came in the PRI? What are their experiences? What are their achievement/future plans? How they are perceived by the others? This chapter is an attempt to review only few among many such studies. However, in spite of being limited in number and scope, these studies provide a comprehensive picture of Panchayat – dalit and tribal interface. Some of the studies reviewed here are the following:

Murthy (1969) found that if the *Sarpanch*, who holds a key position in executing the schemes for Scheduled Castes and Scheduled Tribes, is directly elected by the people and not indirectly by the members of the panchayat, then the interests of scheduled castes and scheduled tribes can be secured better. He has made another important observation with regard to the utilization of resources: the specific funds allotted for the amelioration of SCs and STs under the jurisdiction of Panchayat Samitis have usually been merged with other funds and directed for different purposes.

Parvathamma (1975) analyzed the impact of PRI on weaker sections. One of her observations is that political representation has not helped to bring about the desired level of development among the SCs. She contends that there are built-in drawbacks which present the people of these categories from becoming vocal and assertive and much less to mobilize. To quote her "Poverty, ignorance, illiteracy, the near total dependence on upper castes and above all the lowest ritual rank which makes them a constant source of pollution to caste Hindus certainly limits the scope of the roles they could play as panchayat members."

Ali's (1964) report points out that by and large, the PRI have not been able to devote any special attention and render any significant help to weaker sections mostly due to limited financial resources. Under the existing circumstances and limitations, PRIs have not exhibited any special solicitude for the welfare of the weaker sections of the community.

Gurumurthy (1987) pointed out that the participation of weaker sections as Panchayati Raj functionaries at the village level is not satisfactory. They continued to be passive participants in its meetings and proceedings. This is because they lacked the essential requisites of participation like education and sufficient income.

Adiseshaiah (1964) observed that the involvement of Pradhans in the implementation of schemes has given scope for corruption. As a result, the actual beneficiaries do not get their due and only those beneficiaries who aligned with the pradhans receive some benefits. Even schemes, which were meant for the SCs are manipulated in favour of those who are close to the Pradhans. The most deserving cases remained deprived of the benefits of such development schemes. This became possible because of the in-built scope for manipulations at different levels. The well-to-do pradhans had the capabilities and resources for carrying out such manipulations.

Shymala (2001) conducted study on 594 Zilla Panchayat members in Karnataka, of which 232 were females and 362 males. Specific purpose of the study was to know (a) socio-economic, political and cultural background of the members, and (b) their perceptions and aspirations about the working of panchayats in relation to the expectations of the people and the villagers in general. These are the specific findings:

In case of both males and the females the number of Zilla Panchayat members belonging to more than 50 years of age are very small, but in the case of age upto 30 years the number of female members is much higher than the male members. However, maximum members from both the sexes (40%) are from the age group of 31-40 years. Maximum respondents are Hindus but among them are either from the dominant castes

(29%) or from the scheduled castes (20%). The number of illiterate is much lower (1.34%) but the number of graduates and above, in the case of both the sexes, is much higher (33%). About 5 per cent members are wage earners and 70 per cent are the cultivators. The members are from the land owner families. While about 7 per cent are from the landless category, about 36 per cent members own more than 10 acres of land. But about 38 per cent members are from below the poverty line.

Large number of members (68%) have political experience, but disparity exists in terms of sex because in contrary to 82 per cent males only 47 per cent females have that experience. Social service, welfare of the weaker sections etc. were the main motive behind entering the PRI. The respondents received help of both formal and informal sources to win the election. However, formal sources were more important than the informal. So far as development work is concerned, most of them (48% and 36%) have concentrated on welfare and infrastructural development activities respectively. Although 70 per cent come from farming background, only 9 per cent representatives have done work exclusively for agricultural development. However, the author did not give explanation to this phenomenon. Further, no effort was made to test the validity of the responses pertaining to performance of the respondents as shared by them.

The study by Sheshadri and Azim (2001) was conducted in three villages of Karnataka state. Besides other, one of the objectives of this study was to know the level of awareness of the panchayat functionaries about different schemes/rights accorded to them. The study was conducted on 100 respondents. The findings, in relation to the above issues, reveal that (a) awareness about sources of finance, standing committees, plan, schemes is reasonably high. But they are totally ignorant of the control plan schemes. Further, their participation rate in decision making, planning process and programme monitoring are high but they do not know the rights and importance of *Gram Sabha*. The author also observed that the effect of training at the grassroots level has been limited to creating awareness and inducing participation among PR functionaries, it has not been successful in conscientizing them to become fully functional, (b) the process of transfer of power to the people at the grassroots level has begun. The reservation policy has altered the rural power structure in favour of the marginalised. The new generation has started participating in the activities of PRIs. This does not mean that one can afford to be complacent. The new entrants have yet to acquire the knowledge and skills required to become meaningfully functional. Quite a few of them have been only mouthpieces of stronger sections, given the andro-centric nature of the society, it is more so in the case of women. *Gram Sabha*, is yet to go a long way to play its decisive role.

The study is interesting but it did not cover the social profile of the panchayat functionaries. Further, it is failed to suggest how the functioning of *Gram Sabha* may be ensured.

In other study in the past Aziz (1994) found more or less the same phenomena. While dealing with the relationship between local level traditional power structure, Panchayati Raj and the dalits he said, "attempt made to access power to weaker sections by reserving seats and executive positions have altered hitherto dominant caste centred rural power structure. It should now go to the credit of the makers of law to have given seats and executive positions to the extent of 18 per cent to SC and ST candidates and 33.3 per cent each to backward communities and women. However, since most of the elected representatives are first generation politicians there is a need for providing training to them." (pp. 132-47)

Singh (1985) observed that in the case of U.P. most of the rural leaders of scheduled castes are now young and literate and hail from dominant caste and well to do families amongst their caste groups. Their exposure to mass media, political awareness and political participation is on the increase, but it cannot be rated as very high or satisfactory, which may be the consequences of their socio-economic backwardness. Their entry to the power and authority structure is by and large moved through the process of reservations. But it would be wrong to say that they cannot share power otherwise. Some of them are emerging as leaders by contesting unreserved seats also. This reflects that they are fitting into the larger political processes in the body politics. But their emergence as successful leaders depends upon the group support structure they have. Generally only those persons are able to emerge as leaders who have strong caste, kin and village factional bases. From the point of view of social values they stand half-way between tradition and modernity; they are highly development oriented but feel helpless and are not able to do much because of the oppressive attitudes of the higher castes and classes. Again they are quite responsive to the people of SCs but feel dissatisfied with the role and attitude of the leaders of their own castes and communities. On the whole the findings lend credence to the hypothesis that instead of continuing the old and traditional, the leadership emerging among SCs is new and development oriented and mobility oriented and large sections of them belong to landless working class.

Kanango (1996) discusses Women's leadership in the Panchayati Raj with special reference to the state of West Bengal. The main purpose of this paper is to examine women's leadership in the political arena in the background of the 73rd Constitutional amendment. The author observed that all women candidates were not necessarily formal members of political parties. Different parties identified some female relations of male members and nominated them. Another factor for selecting women candidates is their background and training in different areas. For example, quite a few *Anganwadi* workers got nomination and got elected too. It was also seen that women instructors of Adult Literacy Centres were selected for nomination. Besides, many of the women candidates had undergone a number of training under TRYSEM, DWCRA and some other programmes carried out by the Development Block.

Women entered in Panchayat politics for various reasons. Some entered because they were asked by the party, but some entered in order to get high status. Women representatives also face difficulties. One of the representatives said "Spoke in the meetings about the needs of my area. Had been attending the meetings quite regularly in the beginning but the menfolks do not pay any attention to what I say, do not give any importance. What is the point in attending meetings when I cannot do anything for the people of my area? So I have stopped attending the panchayat meetings since the last six months."

Socio-cultural factors are also acting as a deterrent in many cases. For example, at night if any emergency arises, women obviously are not allowed to go to the spot and help. Even during the day many families object to their going out to settle any dispute among the villagers. Rather their husbands are made to do the job. Apart from attending official meetings at the panchayat or *Panchayat-Samiti* parents'/in-laws'/husband's permission is necessary to visit any other place.

The author concluded that besides various socio-cultural deterrent the effective participation of women in panchayat may be increased provided they attend training programme on regular basis, mindset of all the political parties are made favourable to them and women's organizations put constant pressure on society for its favour.

Pai (1998) studied the functioning of *Pradhans* in the villages in the district of Meerut in Western U.P. All the Panchayat representatives were dalit. She found that reservation alone cannot change the status of women in the family and society and thereby ensure their participation in local bodies. The study also shows that rise in family income and improved lifestyle due to better educational qualification, or investment in business by the male members does not make a difference. The position of women and the perception that they have little knowledge about politics and are incapable of taking part in public affairs, even of independent voting, remain strong. The *Pradhanis* in sampled villagers are mere name sake representatives for the male members of their households. The author added that economic development due to green revolution and market economy has improved income of the sampled households tremendously but have introduced little changes in the social status of women members. On being questioned, all the *Pradhans* said they had agreed to stand for election due to family pressure and the decision of their community, and not because they were keen to do so. All the *Pradhanis* were illiterates and only able to put their signatures on official papers. All of them looked upon the Panchayat as a government organization run by officials and participation by the villagers was seen as unnecessary. Finally, Pai suggested that in order to empower these representatives there is, besides reservation, need to develop not only participatory mechanism of empowerment, but also the means to overcome the structural inequalities of social power. However, without promoting female literacy, independent voting rights, improvement in their status within the family, their proper participation in public sphere may not be ensured.

Mahipal (1998) studied the problems of 651 women Panchayat representatives of all the levels. These women were from U.P. Most of these representatives were dalit, illiterate and poor. He could narrate twelve problems narrated by these women. These were the following :

(a) majority of respondents are not informed about the schemes and the proposed meetings at the Block level. Even if they are informed, in most of the cases they are not allowed by the male family members to attend it. One of the respondents said that "They once went to the Block office to cast their votes in the election of the *Pramukh*. Except that they do not know what role they have in PRIs."
(b) they added that for economic purpose they have to depend on their husbands,
(c) due to fear of above they do not allow girls to attend schools located outside the village,
(d) they are denied *Patta* of their land which they are cultivating since long,
(e) malfunctioning of the PHCs or its poor management,
(f) no improvement in drainage and drinking water facility,
(g) malfunctioning/favouritism in public distribution system shop,
(h) lack of toilet and other essential facility at the place of meeting at Block office,
(i) no-confidence motions against women *Pradhans* are moved in number of GPs. As a result functioning of GP has been affected, GP is failed to mobilizes its own resources because as soon as it imposes taxes, it is opposed by the villagers.

It was found that bureaucracy was not cooperative in empowering the women. It feels superior to the elected representatives of the panchayats. To quote the author,

> "No confidence motions against *Dalit* Women *Pradhans* were moved in a number of *Gram Panchayats*. This shows the power got by weaker sections through Panchayat is not acceptable to the dominant sections of rural society." (p. 151)

On the basis of analysis of problems of women representatives experienced at work the author suggested that just by extending reservation facility women cannot be empowered. For making them empowered it is essential that they need serious training and orientation. It was also suggested that there is low rate of literacy among the elected representatives. This leads to their dependence on husband/secretary. In return these women are forced to remain dependent. In order to make them economically self-reliant they should be encouraged to engage themselves in home based economic activities.

Buch, Jain and Chaudhary (1999) conducted study on women in Panchayati Raj in Madhya Pradesh. The study was conducted in three distinct socio-cultural zones where the ST, SC and others are numerically dominant. So far as their social profile is concerned, the study documented that maximum number of PRI leaders (307 out of 343) are from the marginalised groups. 283 women and 80 men participated in the study. Majority of the leaders are above the age of 25 years. They are engaged in agricultural work. In fact, either they are the wage earners or cultivators. Although, there is slight districtwise variation but majority of the respondents are from below the poverty line. More than 50 per cent are illiterate. Even in the case of chairpersons out of 72, 23 are illiterate. Most of them had no affiliation with any of the political parties in the formal sense. 53 respondents are landless but a good number of them (126) possess either or more than 5 acres of land. It is interesting to note that a good number of respondents have discontinued labour work after becoming PRI leaders but even today 92 are engaged in this work. The study concluded that PRI is numerically dominated by the leaders of lower Socio-economic status in M.P.

Nayak (1996) studied the nature and extent of violence against the panchayat representative of Dalit community. Citing the case of stripping of Draupadi Bai, a Dalit Sarpanch of

Rajgarh district (M.P.) before the BDO on November 19, 1995 the author mentioned that during 1994 election she along with three other women contested the election. The panchayat was reserved for ST women. She defeated the contestants who were Congress supporters. Draupadi is literate, 50 years old poor woman. M. Agarawal (42) was one of the immigrants inhabitants in the village. He belonged to the rich family, but he was a dull man. He had extramarital relation with Bunda Bai (ST). He wanted to get Bunda elected as *Sarpanch* so as to control the Panchayat fund. But it did not materialized. She was defeated. From the date of defeat of Bunda onward Agarwal begins to search opportunity to humiliate Draupadi. In the meantime he succeeded in getting a contract to construct a school building with the help of a non-tribal Panch. He made allegation of misuse of fund against Draupadi. No-confidence motion was brought against her. In that meeting she was badly humiliated/abused even before the pressure of BDO and other officials. At 2 a.m. she tried to escape from the meeting but Agarwal and others pulled her *Sari* and she felled.

Datta (1997) studied the nature of relationship between the established upper caste leadership and the emerging *Dalit* leadership in Panchayat. He is of the view that in spite of prolonged backwardness and economic dependence, the poor *Dalits* may replace the rich leadership of the upper castes, if they are united, assertive and dedicated. The victory of Maiah Wankhede (SC woman) as sarpanch prove this proposition. She herself is an upper caste, educated and urban based woman. But she got married with a dalit activist. When she heard that the panchayat was reserved for women candidates, she decided to contest the election. But the opponent was from a well-to-do family, the family which had dominated the local politics since last 30 years. In spite of all ethical and non-ethical means adopted by the powerful opponent, she won the election only because (a) she and her panel promised the villagers that it will solve the problem of water, toilet and fuel which is faced by the majority, (b) they wrote slogans on walls of each of the houses in the village. In fact not a single wall was left for the opposition to write on. The opposition adopted different techniques. They used and manipulated family pressure, money, liquor, political institution and traditions to win the battle. But they did not succeed.

Pai (2001) studied the role of social capital and panchayat activities in the empowerment of dalits in two district of U.P. state. She observed that since the process of social capital formation is fast and relatively successful in Meerut district of western U.P. than Azamgarh district of eastern U.P., therefore, the role of Gram Panchayat is relatively effective and successful in the former incomparison to the latter. Of course, due to reservation facility the number of Panchayat representatives is high in both the districts, but in the real sense there is radical change in the power structure in the Meerut district but it is not so in the case of Azamgarh. In the latter there is still dominance of upper caste and upper backward caste people in the Panchayat, in spite of the fact that the formal leadership is in the hands of the dalit. It is because the dalit leaders lack social capital. But in Meerut Dalit leaders have very high bargaining power. They either dominate in the Panchayat activities or they negotiate with the local dominant castes like Thakurs and the Jats. Hence, the author rightly concluded that "In Meerut district, closer ties and stronger bonds of social capital have emerged among the Jatavs that has enabled them to challenge the dominance of the Jats and Rajputs, gain control over the panchayats and more benefits from the AVP, though this has created open conflict with the MBCs and other subcastes of dalits. In Azamgarh district, the dalit remain economically weak, with divisions even among the Chamars and unable to collectively challenge the power of Kurmis and Yadavs and play a more effective role in the panchayats. The pace of economic change and political mobilization among the dalits has been much slower in east U.P., creating lower levels of conflict and maintaining existing structure of dominance." (p. 652)

Similar observation was made by Lele (2001). In course of the comparative study between traditional village Panchayat and the modern *Gram Sabha* in Maharashtra from the point of view of empowerment of the weaker sections, the author opined that of course platform of statutory *Gram Sabha* is theoretically opened for the marginalised but in the real sense it is not. In fact, alienation from the political processes seems to prevail and that is why even reservation has not helped to make the marginalised more vocal. This then creates the right conditions for the domination of traditional power of the upper castes and classes. The other factor is economic dependence of the marginalised on the dominants. For those who work on the fields or run small shops or are service providers, opposing the *gavki* is unthinkable. They would be digging their own graves by opposing the upper castes and rich farmers on whose fields they work and earn their daily wages. Besides, personal loans are also made available by the same people, those who constitute the *gavki*. Thus opposing the *gavki* could mean starvation as a result of boycott by the rich peasants and others. (p. 4703)

Pundir (1995) conducted a study in four areas located in eastern and western parts of UP to know (a) to what extent the scheduled castes have been participating in the political process? and (b) whether this participation is leading to participation in decision making? The four areas where the study was conducted are different to each other from the point of view of socio-economic conditions of the dalits. For example, in situation 'a' the scheduled caste is numerically superior, they are occupationally diversified and economically independent. They are a bit modernized. In situation 'b' they are more than 20 per cent population and neither high nor low. In the situation 'c' the SC is politically developed. They organize and consolidate the other scheduled castes for their common cause. The situation 'd' is from the eastern U.P. Here the dalits only participate in voting. There is very less degree of organization of the scheduled castes even for their own affairs. In response to the above two questions the following scenario emerged

1. The scheduled caste is participating in the political processes to a large extent at the local level and has achieved positions of members, somewhere also the highest power position. As members, largely they go on the basis of reservation of seats and also on general seats exceptionally.
2. The SC members and the highest position holders participate in the decision making to a large extent and influence to some extent, also influence in their favour. This is also generating self-confidence and efficacy among them to some extent. But

the extent of this decision making and efficacious participation is not the same in all the above four situations. Actually where there is numerical superiority of SC population and they are economically and occupationally independent, in that situation the extent and nature of political participation is excellent. The numerical strength alone is not sufficient. Since in the situation 'd' there is almost lack of social capital the level of participation is low. Hence, conclusion of Pundir is more or less similar to the conclusion of Pai.

On the basis of review of these few studies it is apparent that almost all the scholars have found reservation facility as the major social intervention to empower the Panchayat representatives belonging to the marginalised section. They have observed that without this facility it would have been rather impossible for them to join PRI. But at the level of their effective participation in decision making as well as in formulation and implementation of the schemes, situation is not very encouraging. The single factor inhibiting these representatives at different levels is the particularistic socio-political environment coupled with near absence of social capitals with them. But in spite of the structural constraints many of them have done wonderful job. A section of them have brought difference in society. Few of them have also paid the price of their assertiveness. The scholars have examined reasons to join PRI, support to win the election, experiences, impact of training programme etc. But the total process and stages involved in the election, their linkages with local and micro level institutions/politicians, cooperation and inhibition, change in attitude, perception motivation and future plan, perception of others about the functioning of the PRI etc., have either been forgotten or have received only passing reference. In this backdrop the present study aims to examine PRI through the eyes of tribal/dalit leaders and assess their experience, aspirations and coping mechanisms.

3

Dalit Leadership in Panchayats

I

METHODOLOGY

Objectives

The study was conducted to achieve the following specific objectives

- to examine social and economic profile of the dalit representatives at all the three levels of Panchayat;
- to find out sources of information of dalit leaders and level of awareness regarding different features of 73rd Constitutional amendment;
- to trace the inhibiting/facilitating factors experienced by the dalit leaders in the day to day functioning;
- to understand the role of reservation/training programme and NGO intervention in the empowerment of dalit representatives;
- to map overall achievements/non-achievements of panchayat headed by dalit representatives;
- to trace major problems of dalit community as perceived by the dalit leaders and the curative efforts made by these leaders in this direction;
- to see the perception of "others" about the functioning and achievements of dalit representatives particularly with reference to their own empowerment as well as the empowerment of dalit masses; and

- to comprehend the opinions of dalit and non-dalit leaders and others essential for the empowerment of common dalits and the dalit leaders.

Universe

Sehore is located on Bhopal-Indore National Highway at a distance of 39 km, from Bhopal. The district is surrounded by Bhopal in north, Raisen in east, Hosangabad in south-east, Sajapur in north-west and Dewas in west. There are five *Tehsils*, five Development Blocks, Sixteen revenue inspector mandals, fourteen police stations, nine police sub-stations, 450 gram panchayats and five JP Panchayats. The population of the district is 10,78,769 (1991) which consists of 1.79 per cent of the State population. The sex ratio is 908. The population growth rate in the district is 28.22. Further, 20.30 and 10.18 per cent of the population (1991) is of SCs and STs respectively. It is needless to mention that *Dhobi, Nai, Chamar* constitute the major population of Scheduled Castes. *Mewara* and *Kahti* are the OBCs. They are physically strong and most of them do agricultural work. Many of the big landowners come from these two castes. *Rajput, Brahmin, Kayastha* and *Baniya* are from the upper castes. The area is also inhabited by *Muslims*. Both *Mewara* and *Khati* are immigrant population from Rajasthan. There is struggle for hegemony between these two castes. *Dal-bati* is their main food item. It is observed that the area under study is full of several problems like, child marriage, *Pardah* system, shortage of drinking water, drop-out among girl students and untochability so on. It is needless to mention that there are large number of *Hindu* temples in the area. Most of these temples have been constructed during last 5 years. There is competition among the villagers to construct good quality and costly temples. These temples are constructed by the upper and backward castes and in many cases dalits are not allowed in these temples. Partly because of unassertiveness and partly in order to avoid conflict in many of the cases dalit themselves do not assert for temple entry.

As per 2001 Census report literacy rate in the district is 63.83 per cent, i.e. 78.14 per cent among men and 47.95 per cent among women. The general description about the district is mentioned below :

Table 3.1 : General information about the district

S. No.	Head	Item/Number	1999-2000	2000-2001
1.	**Climate and geographical Condition**			
	1. Longitude	Degree	22.32-25.40	22.32-25.40
	2. Latitude	Degree	76.22-78.03	76.22-78.03
	3. Height from sea level	Feet	1500-2000	1500-2000
	4. Average rainfall	M.M.	1422.80	529.8
	5. Temperature			
	Maximum	Centigrade	44.5	44.5
	Minimum	Centigrade	4.0	2.5
2.	**Area and Population**			
	1. Geographical area	Sq. km.	6578	6578
	2. Forest area	Sq. km.	1526.63	1526.63
	3. No. of villages	Number	1072	1072
	4. Forest villages	Number	35	35
	5. Inhabited villages	Number	1011	1011
	6. Uninhabited villages	Number	61	61
	7. Tehsil	Number	5	5
	8. JP Panchayat			
	Development Block	Number	5	5
	ST-Development Block	Number	–	–
	9. Town	Number	7	7
	10. Municipal Corporation	Number	–	–
	11. Municipality	Number	2	2
	12. Urban Panchayat	Number	5	5

Source : Obtained from the PRO office, District Magistrate, Sehore, dated 30-11-2002.

As stated, there are 5 Blocks in the district with having 5 JP Panchayats and 450 Gram Panchayat (GP) Panchayats. So far as Sehore block is concerned there are 25 members of which 5 are from the dalit community, at the GP level of 450 Sarpanches the number of SC Sarpanches is 98, of which 67 are male and 31 are female. In the same way there are 1110 GP members of which

173 are from SC of which 143 are males and 30 are females. This is clear from the following table

Table 3.2 : Classification of Z.P. Members on the basis of Caste/Community and Gender (1999)

Block	General		O.B.C.		S.C.		S.T.		Total		Grand Total
	M	F	M	F	M	F	M	F	M	F	
Sehore	1	1	–	1	–	–	1	–	2	2	4
Astha	–	1	1	–	1	1	–	–	2	2	4
Icchawar	–	–	1	–	1	–	–	–	2	–	2
Budhni	1	–	1	–	–	–	–	–	2	–	2
Nasrulla-ganj	1	–	–	–	–	–	–	1	1	1	2
Total	3	2	3	1	2	1	1	1	9	5	14

Classification of J.P. Members on the basis of Caste/Community and Gender (1999)

Block	General		O.B.C.		S.C.		S.T.		Total		Grand Total
	M	F	M	F	M	F	M	F	M	F	
Sehore	9	4	4	2	3	2	1	–	17	8	25
Astha	7	3	4	2	5	3	1	–	17	8	25
Icchawar	5	2	3	2	3	1	2	1	13	6	19
Budhni	5	3	3	1	1	1	2	1	11	6	17
Nasrull-aganj	6	3	3	1	4	2	3	1	16	7	23
Total	32	15	17	8	16	9	9	3	74	35	109

Classification of G.P. Presidents on the basis of Caste/Community and Gender (1999)

Block	General		O.B.C.		S.C.		S.T.		Total		Grand Total
	M	F	M	F	M	F	M	F	M	F	
Sehore	45	22	21	11	16	8	3	1	85	42	127
Astha	33	16	20	11	27	13	3	1	83	41	124
Icchawar	14	8	11	5	9	4	7	4	41	21	62
Budhni	16	9	9	5	5	2	5	5	35	21	56
Nasrulla-ganj	15	8	14	6	10	4	16	8	55	26	81
Total	123	63	75	38	67	31	34	19	299	151	450

Classification of G.P. Members on the basis of Caste/Community and Gender (1999)

Block	General		O.B.C.		S.C.		S.T.		Total		Grand Total
	M	F	M	F	M	F	M	F	M	F	
Sehore	669	347	304	151	224	121	38	13	1235	632	1867
Astha	505	233	262	126	397	180	33	11	1197	550	1747
Icchawar	247	129	105	051	119	062	112	51	0583	293	0876
Budhni	239	126	102	051	066	030	102	46	509	253	0762
Nasrulla-ganj	266	127	130	052	143	030	296	46	835	255	1090
Total	1926	962	903	431	949	423	581	167	4359	1983	6342

Source : Office of District Magistrate, Sehore dated 23-11-02.

On the basis of above table two points are clear, i.e. large number of dalits are found at all the three levels of Panchayat, but like other caste groups among them also men representatives outnumber the women representatives. This shows that even among dalits women have joined PRI only because there is reservation facility for them.

Sampling

The main purpose of the study was to know interface between Panchayat and the dalit leadership. But in order to understand their experience and performance an equal number of non-dalit leaders were also selected. In other words, 12 Sarpanches and 40 Panches were identified. Half of them are dalits. Further from within the dalits and the non-dalits half of them were women. 12 *Gram Sabha* members were also identified to know their views about the functioning/non-functioning of these leaders. The dalit *Gram Sabha* members spoke about the non-dalit headed Panchayat and *vice versa*. In order to bring intensivity and objectivity 4 government officials working at the local level and 4 ZP/JP members were also selected. These members represent the area under study. We also prepared 4 case studies. Hence altogether 76 persons participated in the study. Half of them were dalits and women. This is clear from Table 3.3.

Table 3.3 : Status, Caste and Genderwise description of the respondents

Respondents	Dalit		Non-dalit		Total
	Male	Female	Male	Female	
Sarpanch	3	3	3	3	12
Panch	10	10	10	10	40
Gram Sabha Members	3	3	3	3	12
ZP/JP Members	1	1	1	1	4
Government Officials	1	1	1	1	4
Case Study	1	1	1	1	4
Total	19	19	19	19	76

Instrument

Semi-structured interview schedule was the main instrument of data collection. Different types of interview schedule were administered on the dalit leaders, non-dalit leaders, *Gram Sabha* members and ZP/JP members. On the government officials and NGOs interview guide was used. For case study informal discussion was organized with the selected leaders. Besides these, we also collected factual information from the secondary sources, viz., government records and published literature.

II
PANCHAYAT REPRESENTATIVE: SOCIAL AND ECONOMIC PROFILE

Sehore is one of the districts closely related to state capital in terms of distance (35km) and transport and communication facility. It is divided into 5 *Tehsils* and the area under study, i.e. Sehore is biggest in terms of its population (1,98,287). The study was conducted in Sehore *tehsil*.

Position in PRI

Twenty-eight dalits and 28 non-dalits participated in the study of which 6 Sarpanchs from both the categories, 40 panchs, i.e. 20 dalits and 20 non-dalits were interviewed. From the JP Panchayat level 4 representatives were interviewed. We also interviewed government officials and community members to know their perception about overall functioning of dalit and non-dalit headed gram panchayat and its achievement. Social profile of the respondents and their family members are separately mentioned below.

Structure of House

Out of 28 dalit representatives, 24 are living in *kachha* houses, but in contrary to this of 28 non-dalit representatives only 11 are living in *kachha* houses. Similarly there are 6 non-dalit representatives who have *puckka* houses, but not even a single dalit representative have such type of house. This shows that maximum number of the respondents who participated in the study are from lower economic status.

Profile of the Respondents

Most of the dalit respondents are middle aged, married and illiterate. They are engaged in the wage work and therefore, majority of them (82%) are from below the poverty line. In contrary to this majority of the respondents from the non-dalit category are of course from the middle age and married but they are educated, engaged in the agricultural work and 32 per cent of them have annual income of more than Rs. 20,000. This is clear from Table 3.4.

Profile of Family Members (Including Respondents)

More or less in the case of dalit and non-dalit representatives family size is similar in terms of number and also in terms of sex-ratio but in both the cases women slightly outnumber the male population.

Age

In both the cases the number of children and young family members is much higher in comparison to the adult and the senior citizen. For example, upto the age of 9 years there are 55

Table 3.4 : Profile of the Respondents

Age-Group	Dalit		Non- Dalit	
	Frequency	Per cent	Frequency	Per cent
15-24	4	14	1	4
25-34	10	36	10	36
34-44	8	28	10	36
45-59	3	11	6	20
60+	3	11	1	4
Total	28	100	28	100
Marital Status				
Unmarried	3	10	—	—
Married	21	75	27	96
Divorced	4	15	1	4
Total	28	100	28	100
Education				
Illiterate	9	33	9	32
Literate	7	25	7	25
Primary	5	18	5	18
Middle	4	12	4	12
Matric	2	8	2	8
U.G./P.G.	1	4	1	4
Total	28	100	28	100
Occupation				
Nothing	4	12	4	12
Labour	8	29	8	29
Agriculture	5	18	5	18
Labour+Agri.	8	29	8	29
Private Job	2	8	2	8
Others	1	4	1	4
Total	28	100	28	100
Annual Income				
Nothing	3	11	3	11
Upto 5000	3	11	3	11
5000-10000	17	60	17	60
10000-20000	2	7	2	7
20000+	3	11	3	11
Total	28	100	28	100

children among the dalit families, but the number of children in this age group is 38 in the case of non-dalit households. But in the higher age groups the number of members have drastically decreased but the pattern of decrease is relatively slow in the case of non-dalit families. There are 8 senior citizens in the case of dalit households and 10 in the case of non-dalit households. This is clear from Table 3.4.

Marital Status

The number of unmarried persons is much higher (27) among the dalits in comparison to the non-dalits. But the number of married persons is much higher among the non-dalits (98) in comparison to the dalits (60). There are very few divorced or widow / widower among both the type of households.

Education

The number of illiterate is higher among dalits in comparison to non-dalits. But the number of matriculates and college educated persons is much higher among the non-dalits in comparison to the dalits. Hence, as the level of education increases, particularly beyond the stage of matriculation, the number of beneficiaries decreases but the rate of decrease is much higher among the dalits in comparison to the non-dalits.

Occupation

In both the cases agriculture related work is the main source of livelihood. Within agriculture work the family members are differently related to land. While there are 48 persons from the dalit category, who are working as agriculturist or wage labour or both, but in the case of non-dalits hardly 3 persons are wage earners. Fourty-three are agriculturists and about 12 persons are partly agriculturists and partly wage workers. None of the members from dalit community are engaged in business or government job. There are 8 persons from the non-dalit community engaged in both these non-agricultural occupations.

Annual Income

In terms of income also there is clear difference between the dalit and the non-dalit households. For example, there are 51 persons from the dalit category whose annual income is less than

Rs. 10000 but in this income group the number of non-dalit members is only 28. Similarly there are only 4 dalit households whose annual income is above Rs. 20000 but there are 27 non-dalits, who fall in this vary income group.

Table 3.5 : Profile of respondents and family members

Sex	Dalit		Non-Dalit	
	Frequency	Per cent	Frequency	Per cent
Male	80	50	87	49
Female	81	50	89	51
Total	161	100	176	100
Age-Group				
0-9	55	34	38	22
10-14	20	12	19	11
15-24	29	18	34	19
25-34	28	17	33	19
34-44	15	9	19	11
45-59	6	4	23	13
60+	8	5	10	6
Total	161	100	176	100
Marital Status				
Not Applicable	68	42	64	36
Unmarried	27	17	10	6
Married	60	37	98	56
Divorced	1	1	0	0
Widow/ Widower	5	3	4	2
Total	161	100	176	100
Education				
Not Applicable	29	18	17	10
Illiterate	33	20	25	14
Literate	14	9	8	5
Primary	50	31	50	28
Middle	27	17	30	17
Matric	7	4	36	20
U.G./P.G.	1	1	10	6
Total	161	100	176	100
Occupation				
Nothing	53	33	78	44
Not Applicable	49	30	30	17

(Contd.)

Table 3.5 (Contd.)

	Dalit		Non-Dalit	
	Frequency	Per cent	Frequency	Per cent
Labour	28	17	3	2
Agriculture	9	6	43	24
Labour+ Agri.	18	11	12	7
Private Job	3	2	2	1
Business	0	0	6	3
Govt. Job	0	0	2	1
Others	1	1	0	0
Total	161	100	176	100
Annual Income				
Not Applicable	102	63	113	64
Upto 5000	9	6	8	5
5000-10000	42	26	20	11
10000-20000	4	2	8	5
20000+	4	2	27	15
Total	161	100	176	100

Membership in Political Party

Respondents from both the categories are exposed to the political activity. But its possibility is relatively higher among the non-dalits. For instance, of 28 dalit representatives 12 and of 28 non-dalit representatives 17 are members of political parties. They are the members since long. This is because out of 12 members from dalits and out of 17 from non-dalits 10 and 13 respectively are the members of political parties from before 1990. This shows the root of politics in the rural areas of Sehore. Most of them, from both the categories, are the members of Congress Party. However, the data reveal that few of them are the members of BJP and this party is relatively more popular among the non-dalits. None of the dalit representatives have any association with BSP. So far as their father's association with political party is concerned among the dalits many of them (20) said that their parents had nothing to do with any of the political party. But among the non-dalits fathers of significant number of respondents (46%) had association with political party. Here also in both the cases Congress Party is more popular in comparison to the BJP.

So far as nature of participation in political activities, except voting, is concerned, majority of the respondents from both the categories never participated in *Dharna* or fast. Only 4 Panchayat representatives from non-dalit category participated in *Dharna* in the past. In the same way very few of them, i.e. 3 from dalit, and 5 from non-dalit category respondents are currently associated with any of the social organizations. It is needless to mention that in the area under study there are several NGOs/cultural bodies since last few years, but majority of the respondents are not associated with these organizations. However, some of the respondents are associated with *Samarthan, Kabir Panth, Jansattha Dugdha Sangh* and *Rastriya Samaj Prakoshta.* They are associated with these organizations and their activities as a social worker or propagator.

Change in Social Status

Irrespective of social background of persons once they associated themselves with social and political organizations, there is a possibility of impact of the new assignment on their status either positively or negatively. In this case also one can see such impact. But in the case of both there is improvement in social status of large number of respondents, i.e. 18 each from both the categories. Some people also feel that they have lost wage work because of this assignment. Similarly some do not perceive any change in their status. One of the dalit respondents said that most often people laugh on him and therefore, he feels humiliated. This is clear from the following Table 3.6.

Table 3.6 : Improvement in status/supporters increased?

S. No.	Response	Dalit		Non-Dalit	
		Frequency	Per cent	Frequency	Per cent
1	Social Status improved	18	64	18	64
2	Number of supporter increased	1	4	1	4
3	No Change	7	24	6	21
4	Social Status decreased	0	0	1	4
5	Became famous	0	0	1	4
6	Loss of work	1	4	0	0
7	People laugh on me	1	4	0	0
8	1+2	0	0	1	4
	Total	28	100	28	100

Land and Irrigation Facility

Many of the dalit representatives are landless. It was found that while the number of landless is 2 among the non-dalits the same is 10 among the dalits. Further, the area of land owned by the dalit land owner is low. For instance, 11 dalits have less than 2.5 acres of land but in this category there are only 2 respondents from the non-dalit category. In contrary to this, there are 8 respondents from the non-dalit category who possess more than 10 acres of land but there is not even a single dalit respondent in this vary category. This shows that in the area under study land is mainly in the hands of non-dalits. This is clear from the following Table 3.7.

Table 3.7 : Land holding size

S. No.	Response	Dalit		Non-Dalit	
		Frequency	Per cent	Frequency	Per cent
1	Landless	10	36	2	7
2	Upto 2.5 acres	11	39	2	7
3	2.5 to 5 Acres	4	14	8	29
4	5 to 10 Acres	3	11	8	29
5	10 Acres +	0	0	8	29
	Total	28	100	28	100

So far as categorization of land in terms of availability of irrigation facility is concerned in the case of both, the condition of irrigation is not upto the mark. However, well and tube-well and both the facilities are relatively more common among the non-dalits than the dalits. For instance, 5 dalits have facility of well and tube-well for irrigation but there are 18 non-dalits who have this facility.

Indebtedness

Indebtedness is found among both the dalit and the non-dalit representatives. There are 16 dalits and 14 non-dalits who are under debt. However, more dalits take loan from local *sahukar* and more non-dalits take loan from formal organizations like banks and cooperative bodies. Further, the purpose of loan is also different among them. For instance, most of the non-dalits take loan for agricultural development, but most of the dalit representatives take loan to meet social expenditure like food, marriage, treatment or the combination of all. In an earlier study the author (Chaudhary: 2002) found similar situation among the tribes of Jhabua and Betul districts. Jhabua is underdeveloped area with degraded land. Here the tribals take loan from the informal sources mainly for consumption purpose. The rate of return is very low. In contrary to this the tribals of Betul live in the relatively developed area. In this area the condition of forest and agricultural land is better. They take loan from the formal sources. The main purpose behind loan is to improve agricultural operation. Therefore, the rate of return is much higher.

Saving

Very few of the respondents have saving. However, the amount of saving is much higher among the non-dalits than the dalits. For instance, all the 3 dalit representatives who have saving, they have saved less than Rs.5000 each. But there are 14 non-dalits who have saving and 2 of them have the saving of more than Rs. 5000. Hence, it is clear that the intensity of indebtedness is high among the dalits and intensity of saving is higher among the non-dalits.

Assets

There is clear gap among both the categories of respondents in terms of possession of assets. For instance, so far as basic amenities are concerned, there are 3 dalit and 8 non-dalit households who have telephone facility. Similarly 7 dalits and 15 non-dalits have hand-pump facility. About 43 per cent dalits and 61 per cent non-dalits have toilet facility inside their houses. But drawing room facility is not very popular among the dalits but barring few all the respondents have the facility of electricity in their houses.

So far as availability of agricultural and other assets are concerned the distinction is very clear. For example, 9 dalits have plough but 22 non-dalits have this facility. Tractor is not with any of the dalits but 9 of the non-dalits have this facility. Similarly there are 15 and 20 non-dalit respondents who have the facility of sprayer and pump-set, but there are hardly 6 dalits who have this facility.

Table 3.8 : Agricultural/Household assets

Agricultural Assets	Dalit						Non-Dalit					
	Frequency			Per cent			Frequency			Per cent		
	Yes	No	Total	Yes	No	Total	Yes	No	Total	Yes	No	Total
Plough	9	19	28	32	68	100	22	6	28	79	21	100
Bullock Cart	5	23	28	18	82	100	15	13	28	54	46	100
Tractor	0	28	28	0	100	100	9	19	28	32	68	100
Thresher	1	27	28	4	96	100	14	14	28	50	50	100
Bullock	7	21	28	25	75	100	22	6	28	79	21	100
Harvester	0	28	28	0	100	100	0	28	28	0	100	100
Sprayer	2	26	28	7	93	100	15	13	28	54	46	100
Pump Set	4	24	28	14	86	100	20	8	28	71	29	100
Household Assets												
Cooler/Fan	11	17	28	39	61	100	24	4	28	86	14	100
Bicycle	7	21	28	25	75	100	22	6	28	79	21	100
Two Wheeler	3	25	28	11	89	100	14	14	28	50	50	100
Four Wheeler	0	28	28	0	100	100	1	27	28	4	96	100
Radio/Tape	10	18	28	36	64	100	19	9	28	68	32	100
T.V.	6	22	28	21	79	100	21	7	28	75	25	100

In terms of household assets the same variation continues. Whether it is the availability of cooler/fan, bicycle or two-wheeler its number is much higher among the non-dalits than the dalits. One non-dalit has four-wheeler but it is not with any of the dalits. Similarly television is available with 6 dalits and 21 non-dalits. This is clear from Table 3.8.

On the basis of above analysis it is clear that whether it is the structure of house, education, marital status, annual income, membership of political party, availability of land, sources of irrigation, amount of saving and agricultural and household assets everything is possessed more by the non-dalits than dalits. In other words, in the light of the 73rd Constitutional amendment, the new PRI was introduced at that very time also the nature of dalit and the non-dalit participation was quite dissimilar to each other. Under the given unequal state of affairs how and to what extent both the dalit and the non-dalit panchayat representatives participate in the panchayat activities needs to be probed. Do they have common response and performance? Are they equally facing problem or receive support is an issue which have been addressed in the following sections.

III

PANCHAYAT REPRESENTATIVES AND THEIR LEVEL OF AWARENESS

Level of awareness is directly related to use or adoption of development schemes. It helps people to form opinion and regulate behaviour pattern in relatively proper direction. It is true that awareness is not a sufficient condition, but it is also true that without awareness people at large cannot participate and therefore, dream of democracy which is dependent on peoples participation cannot succeed. Awareness is both cause and effect. If the level of education, contact with formal and informal means of communication and association with social organizations is high, the level of awareness is likely to be high. Hence, here awareness is a byproduct of exposure. But it can contribute to people's participation for development and in this case it becomes one of the causes of success or not success of development schemes. Looking to these implications of awareness, in the proposed study, an attempt was made to know sources and level of awareness of panchayat representatives regarding some of the social issues.

Knowledge about Basic Facts

In response to a question that under the 73rd Constitutional amendment in which year the Panchayati Raj was introduced, majority of the respondents, i.e. 21 dalits and 20 non-dalits replied in the negative. In other words, about 75 per cent of the respondents from both the categories do not know when the new PR system was introduced. Only 8 persons had right answer. Seven respondents did not even pass comment on this issue. They do not have even heard amendment.

Why the new PRI was introduced? Some respondents did not respond to this question, but contrary to this others responded. 25 per cent dalits and 21 per cent non-dalits said that this system was introduced for the development of the village. Some respondents replied that it was thought that by introducing the new PRI villagers may be made self-reliant in terms of development and solution of their problems. Three non-dalit respondents said that for political mileage this scheme was introduced by the governing political party. Kamal Singh Parihar, an upper caste panch of Lasuria Parihar Panchayat said, "The new PRI will translate dream of Gandhiji into action. People will praise the government and will cast vote in its favour." But the dalits did not respond to this question. In contrary to this, about 14 per cent dalit respondents said that this scheme was introduced for more than one purpose such as for village development, construction work in village and solution of the villagers' problem in the village itself, but none of the non-dalit respondents referred to these issues. This is clear from Table 3.9.

Table 3.9 : Objective of New PRI as perceived by the respondents

S. No	Response	Dalit		Non-Dalit	
		Frequency	Per cent	Frequency	Per cent
1	No Response	7	25	6	21
2	Total Development	4	14	2	7
3	Village Development	7	25	6	21
4	Construction in village	1	4	2	7
5	Panchayat should take care of village	–	–	2	7
6	Social Justice/Poor's Welfare	1	4	–	–
7	Awareness	1	4	–	–
8	Villagers work in village itself	3	11	3	11
9	Village problem to be solved in village	–	–	2	7
10	Fulfil the dream of Gandhiji	–	–	1	4
11	Political mileage	–	–	2	7
12	Political purpose	–	–	1	4
13	3+4	–	–	1	4
14	2+3+4	2	7	–	–
15	3+5	2	7	–	–
	Total	28	100	28	100

Reservation

Of course there is provision of 33 per cent reservation for women at all the three levels of Panchayati Raj, but for dalits the formula is totally different. There is reservation for them as per their number or numerical strength in their respective district and block. It is amazing to note that of the 28 dalit respondents, 20 do not know that there is specific per cent reservation facility for them in the Panchayati Raj. Many of them also do not know that there is reservation facility for them in all the 8 committees formed under *Gram Sabha* scheme to ensure people's democracy not under the sarpanch, but under the entire village elders. About 53 per cent non-dalit representatives also do not know the exact percentage of reservation for dalits in their respective JP/Gram Panchayat. In fact, a single dalit and 5 non-dalits know the exact percentage of reservation of seats in the panchayat for dalits. Many of the respondents from both the categories (14) did not respond to this question.

More or less, similar is the situation in the case of knowledge about reservation facility for women. To have proper knowledge about reservation facility for women is not complex because right from village up to the district level 33 per cent seats are reserved for them but majority of the dalits (77%) and non-dalits (53%) have wrong information about this facility. Further, many of them are indifferent on this issue. Only 6 respondents have correct information about this facility.

Knowledge about Rights

Panchayat representatives have been conferred different rights and it is expected from them that they should know and exercise these rights. But here also only 32 per cent dalits and 50 per cent non-dalits have information about their legal rights. In other words, 61 per cent dalits and 39 per cent non-dalits do not know about their rights. Unfortunately the training programme either did not reach to them or it did not provide information to them regarding the reservation facility and rights and duties of panchayat representatives. It is needless to mention that success of Panchayati Raj also depends on training to the representatives on constant basis, regarding different social issues. But in this study it was found that 20 dalits and 19 non-dalits have not attended any training programme during last 2 years. Further, 10 respondents from both the categories have attended one training programme. Hence, it is observed that given the lower educational status of panchayat representatives as well as their isolation from training programme, their level of awareness regarding rights and duties are bound to remain low.

Table 3.10 : Educational background of the respondents who attended training programme

Education	Training Programme	
	Dalit	Non-dalit
Illiterate	1	–
Literate	2	2
Primary	1	1
Middle	1	1
Matric	–	1
Total	5	5

Only 10 dalit and 14 non-dalit respondents passed comments on the sufficiency of the rights provided to them. While 4 dalit respondents are satisfied with the rights extended to them, 3 non-dalit respondents feel that it is sufficient. As per their perception 6 dalit and 11 non-dalit respondents feel that these rights are not sufficient to deal with village level problems. They are of the opinion that some more rights should be extended to them. While 18 per cent dalits said that the decision taken in the gram-sabha meeting should be implemented without delay, the non-dalit did not respond to this question. Narayani Bai, Woman Panch of Sikarpur Panchayat said that "Grants released to Panchayat is disproportionately possessed by the sarpanch. The amount should equally be divided for each of the wards. Today the wards represented by the poor panch is neglected in this matter." 5 dalit and non-dalit respondents desired that they must have right to punish the offenders. On other rights such as legalization of rights, equal right to panch and sarpanch etc., representative did not respond. One of the respondents, Taravati (SC sarpanch) said that "There are many laws, but seldom these laws are implemented. It is the rich people who dominate in panchayat. Because of panchayat there is improvement in their social status. Nobody listen to the poor and the dalit representatives. Hence, it is the government which can come forward and ask all the concerned to implement the existing laws and in the case of non-compliance they should be punished. The dalit representatives cannot implement the laws because economically and socially they are not powerful." Sarpanch Achal Singh (Non-dalit) of Thuna Kala Panchayat said that "Power conferred to the Panchayat is not sufficient in the real sense. The decision taken by the *Gram Sabha* and the proposals made out of these decisions are always not owned by the administration. They should not alter/change it, otherwise the Panchayat people feel humiliated."

Duties

Panchayat representatives are directly accountable to the local people and their problems. They are not simply supposed to prepare a list of local problems and pass it on to the higher authority, but they themselves have to deal with the problem in collaboration with the people who are facing these problems. There are 16 persons, i.e. 9 dalits and 7 non-dalits who do not have knowledge about duties. The others have some knowledge, for example, 21 per cent dalit and non-dalit respondents said that the main duty of panchayat representative is to solve the village problem. Significant number of them also expect social development from these representatives.

Source of Information

The villagers live in an informal environment. Most often their source of information is local and informal in nature. In this case, the local sources are in itself not well informed and therefore, in that case these sources cannot provide accurate, broad and intensive information.

So far as source of information regarding election, legal rights and duties etc. are concerned, the following information was obtained from the respondents. Ten dalits and 3 non-dalits came to know about the first and the second election from the villagers. The old panchayat representatives also informed to about 43 per cent respondents. Only few of them were informed by father/husband. The role of television and newspaper etc. is very insignificant. None of the dalit and only 3 non-dalit respondents were informed about election by T.V. and newspaper. In other words, it is observed that both formal and informal sources of information are operative among the dalit and the non-dalit representatives, but the formal source is relatively popular among the non-dalits. So far as information pertaining to rights and duties are concerned in this case the role of panchayat meeting and interaction with villagers is more important. In both types of respondents, the role of training programme is not very popular, because only 4 respondents received information about the rights and duties from this source. This is clear from the following Table 3.11.

Table 3.11 : Source of information

S. No	Response	Dalit		Non-Dalit	
		Frequency	Per cent	Frequency	Per cent
1	No response	4	14	–	–
2	Training	1	4	3	11
3	Panchayat Meeting	8	29	7	25
4	Interaction with villagers	5	18	4	14
5	Not applicable	3	11	5	18
6	Husband	1	4	1	4
7	Gram Sevak	–	–	1	4
8	Self-thinking	2	7	2	7
9	By reading act	–	–	2	7
10	Family members	1	4	–	–
11	Father	–	–	1	4
12	Block office	1	4	1	4
13	3+4	1	4	–	–
14	4+8	1	4	–	–
15	2+12	–	–	1	4
	Total	28	100	28	100

It is true that the level of knowledge about their rights and duties are low, but in course of investigation it was found that 68 per cent dalits and 64 per cent non-dalits felt that their level of knowledge is neither high nor low. Only 2 non-dalit respondents felt that their level of knowledge is very high.

How to enhance the level of awareness in order to make these representatives more informed and more assertive? Respondents gave different suggestions. For example, some respondents feel that training programme should be organized on constant basis. Further, if the panchayat will discharge duties actively and timely the level of knowledge of panchayat and its representatives will definitely increase. Also, if the panchayat representatives are empowered in the functional sense and if these representatives have direct linkage with development agencies, the amount of awareness among the villagers will definitely increase. In other words, panchayat can only show its visibility not by sentimentalizing its people in terms of caste, class and gender but by doing work honestly and timely. If the panchayat is really sensitive and assertive people themselves will realise its importance.

Training Programme

As stated earlier, very few of the respondents till date have attended the training programme and that too for very limited period and for few days only. Therefore, it is doubtful whether during the training the salient features of Panchyati Raj were shared with participants or not. The respondents are of the view that issues of training programme was related to panchayat, agriculture, welfare-work, *gram-swaraj* and environment. These limited number of respondents, i.e. 3 dalits and 4 non-dalits, opined that their level of knowledge have increased after attending the training programme. They also came to know that how village work can be done from inside the village and how self-confidence may be increased. Some respondents acquired new knowledge and skill and they shared it with others.

On the basis of above analysis it is clear that the level of knowledge regarding panchayat election, rights and duties of panchayat representatives, reasons behind introducing the new PRI, the current percentage of reservation, appropriateness of rights, source of information about all these issues are all not above the average in the case of both dalit and non-dalit representatives. However, the condition is more pitiable among the dalit than the non-dalit representatives. The role of communication system, both formal and informal is not visible. Actually the training programme is yet to reach to the large number of representatives. Even those who attended the programme, their level of knowledge is not at all correct and intensive. Besides the content of the training programme, the limited number, hour and days of training programme is also responsible for the low level of awareness.

IV

ACHIEVEMENT AND EXPECTATION

Reservation is one of the pre-conditions to encourage and ensure participation of dalits in panchayat activities. It is a necessary condition because their actual participation depends upon variety of personal and social conditions. Further the social and political environment may be helpful or may not be. Under the given circumstances it is found that in spite of reservation facility many of the dalit representatives have bitter experience and they face difficulties in discharging duties because the social environment, where they are working, is historically not pro-democracy. Non-dalits have also different positive and negative experience with the Panchayati Raj institution depending upon their own personal and environmental conditions. The present section deals with the experiences and strategies of both dalit and non-dalit representatives in terms of their achievements and future expectation.

Dalits in Panchayat

In the past in most of the cases either dalits were not in the panchayat system or if they were their number was few and far between. These few were hardly independent in terms of their role in the panchayat activities. In many of the cases they were either the passive observer or the spokesperson of the local influential. They used to join PRI through cooption. But since the introduction of new PRI after 73rd Constitutional amendment, there are thousands of dalit representatives at all the three levels of panchayat. They have joined PRI through direct election and not through cooption. They are not only members in different committees of *Gram Sabha*, gram panchayat and higher level panchayats, but also they are president of many of these panchayats at all the three levels.

It is obvious that because of variety of local and outside factors the process of class and elite formation is going on among the dalits as it is going on among other castes and caste groups. Once the panchayat or constituency is reserved for dalit then for any elective post-dalit members have to contest and compete only with the dalit members. In that situation the dalit who is relatively more powerful is likely to be elected more incomparison to the less powerful dalits. In response to a question that why the respondent from the dalit community was elected and not the other member of the same caste or caste group 6 did not respond to this question and 6 were elected unopposed. The social reputation of these six elected unopposed is high among the community members. Their caste people perceive them relatively more conscious and active. They thought that by electing them unopposed they can get some common work done smoothly. Achal Singh Mewara a non-dalit sarpanch of Thuna Kala, who defeated a nearest rival candidate by the margin of 428 votes said that "The ex-sarpanch was incompetent to visit Block office regularly and get the work done. He had no technique to convince the officials. People feel happy to elect me. They see ray of hope in me. Therefore, nobody opposed my candidature." Twenty-one per cent respondents said that people preferred them in comparison to other candidates because the latter were rough and unfriendly to the people. Two were elected because of their family reputation. Babulal, non-dalit panch of Raipure Panchayat said that " I was identified and elected by the villagers because I am a young man. People see ray of hope in me. They want many thing from me." But some of the respondents were purely elected due to their personal traits. Two respondents were elected because of both unfriendly behaviour of the opposite candidate as well as their poor family reputation.

Difficulties

Whether being dalit, panchayat representatives face difficulties in doing their panchayat work? 10 respondents do not face such difficulties, 3 said that they have low status in the village therefore, nobody listen to them and 3 members said that since the sarpanch is non-dalit, therefore, he seldom listen to their views. One of the respondents feel that whatever proposal is submitted by him, it is rejected. A Dalit Panch of Lasuria Panchayat, Jai Singh said, "Since Dalits are in less number in Panchayat body, therefore, non-dalit members do not listen to them. We most often oppose their unacceptable views in the meeting unsuccessfully. People from general category dominate in our Panchayat. We as a dalit representative are failed to avail any benefit from the Panchayat body." One of the dalit women sarpanch said that she is unable to get her proposal approved. It is needless to mention that the ex-sarpanch had misappropriated the fund. Therefore, people feel that she will also misuse the fund. In order to overcome this problem, she published her trouble in the local newspaper and also wrote an application disclosing the difficulties to the higher official. But nothing came out in the concrete sense. One dalit said that he is not heard simply because he is illiterate. He said that only those dalits are active and assertive who are powerful. People and the politicians hear only the educated and powerful dalit representatives. Hem Raj Jatav (SC) Panch of Barahgarh Panchayat said "Sarpanch and others only send papers to me for signature. They never inform me to attend any meeting." It is needless to mention that Jatav is a marginal farmer and his family is under debt since long.

In order to overcome the above problem many of the dalits (15) do not take any step. A couple of them on demand do not hesitate to pay bribe to the official in order to get the work completed. But none of these dalit representatives organize themselves, discuss and formulate strategies to overcome problems created by the local and the block level officials at the collective level. Rather in most of the cases they feel that they should be helped by administration, non-dalit representatives and higher level panchayat functionaries.

But this does not mean that they do not receive help from them. Although 20 dalits feel that they do not take help from others, 4 dalits feel that everybody listen to them and whatever is asked by them, both dalit and non-dalit members listen to their voice. One respondent said that the non-dalit just take his signature in the meeting of Gram Sabha. Similarly one respondent receives help as per his own choice.

Help from Others

Both dalit and non-dalit respondents take help from others in their private life. Actually more dalit representatives take help in comparison to the non-dalits. And the nature of help slightly defer. For instance, 9 dalits have taken loan, but only 2 non-dalits have availed this obligation. Some of the respondents also helped each other. There are 8 respondents from both the categories who seek help as per the requirement which may differ from simple guidance to panchayat work and panchayat gram sabha meeting.

Do they feel pressure because of help? None of them feel any pressure because of the above obligation. However, one of the dalit respondents feel pressure. Actually one of his voters who supported him during the time of panchayat election put pressure on him to get his personal work done. Otherwise, neither there is pressure because of help nor they are disturbed because of rare encroachment in the functioning.

But this does not mean that the panchayat representatives are free to take decision in panchayat on the basis of merit of the case. Actually some of the respondents, i.e. 2 dalits and 9 non-dalits feel that they are free to take decision, but large number of them, i.e. 89 per cent dalits and 54 per cent non-dalits are forced to be influenced by others both from within the panchayat body or outside the body to take decision in different manner. Hence, the decisions are not independently taken by both the dalits and the non-dalits. Reasons are the following: 25 per cent dalit and 21 per cent non-dalit feel that they are forced by the decision taken in the meeting of *gram sabha*. In the meeting of the *gram sabha* nobody is accountable to anybody. In the meeting many decisions are taken which cannot be implemented due to shortage of fund. In that situation the elected representatives loose their credit. They are criticized by *gram sabha* without looking into the constraints. Hence, the *gram sabha* members have not to loose vote, therefore, on some occasions it raises issues which are radical in nature. In many cases the sarpanch do not listen to the panch. It is the sarpanch who decide the course of action. This was stated by 12 dalit and 2 non-dalit panches. In the case of one of the dalit women representatives and 2 non-dalit representatives everything is done by their husbands, they just put their signatures. There are 2 representatives who do not attend the meeting but they willingly put signature as and when required. This is clear from the following Table 3.12.

Table 3.12 : Reasons for not taking independent decision

S. No	Response	Dalit		Non-Dalit	
		Frequency	Per cent	Frequency	Per cent
1	No response/no reply	–	–	2	7
2	Not applicable	3	11	12	43
3	Decision by gram sabha meeting	7	25	6	21
4	Sarpanch decides	12	43	2	7
5	Do not visit panchayat office	1	4	–	–
6	Everything done by husband	1	4	2	7
7	Signature without attending meeting	1	4	1	4
8	Decision by the influential	1	4	1	4
9	Nobody listen	–	–	2	7
10	JP members are heard	2	7	–	–
	Total	28	100	28	100

Two dalit representatives said that it is BJP members who take the real decision. Three non-dalits respondents feel that in panchayat body only the influential members are heard.

Work for Dalits Empowerment

Of course some significant works have been done by the respondents for overall development of their respective panchayats, but it is very difficult to say what have been done exclusively for the welfare of dalits. For example, untouchability is in practice in the area under study. But hardly any respondent has done anything to deal with this problem. Actually 15 dalits and 8 non-dalits have done nothing exclusively for the development of dalits. Some of the major works done by a section of the dalit and non-dalit respondents are road construction, house construction under IAY, hand-pump facility, preparation of proposal, management of land related paper.

bridge construction etc. Unfortunately speaking none of these works are exclusively related to the development of dalits.

It is needless to mention that as per the perception of both dalit and non-dalit representatives, some of the specific problems faced by the dalits have neither been addressed by the dalit nor by the non-dalit representatives. As stated above, those who have done some development work they have addressed only general issues like road construction, proposal preparation, bridge construction etc. But the problem of lack of employment opportunity, education facility, problem of migration, drinking water problem, landlessness, loan facility, inclusion of name in BPL list etc. have not been addressed by these representatives. The problem of alcoholism and untouchability has not drawn attention of the representatives.

In order to deal with this problem some specific efforts are required from the representatives. The respondents suggest that the facility of land, loan, road and hand-pump, employment opportunity, name in BPL list, pension, schooling facility etc. should be provided to the dalits so that their quality of life may significantly improve. This is clear from the following Table 3.13.

Table 3.13 : Problems of dalits

S. No.	Response	Dalit		Non-Dalit	
		Frequency	Per cent	Frequency	Per cent
1	No response	1	4	–	–
2	Lack of school	1	4	2	–
3	Lack of employment opportunity	4	14	3	11
4	Physical movement	4	14	–	–
5	Drinking water problem/electricity/latrine	3	11	–	–
6	Land	2	7	–	–
7	Loan	1	4	–	–
8	Inclusion in BPL list	1	4	–	–
9	Pension	–	–	2	7
10	Alcoholism	–	–	1	4
11	Road/Drainage	–	–	1	4
12	No problem	–	4	4	14
13	Do not get benefits from schemes	1	4	–	–
14	2+3+5+13	2	7	–	–

(Contd.)

Table 3.13 (Contd.)

15	3+4+11+12	1	4	–	–
16	3+5+9	1	4	–	4
17	3+7+12	1	4	–	–
18	3+7+10+11	1	4	–	–
19	5+15	1	4	–	14
20	6+7	1	4	2	7
21	6+8	1	4	1	4
	Total	28	100	28	100

Problems with Dalit Community

One of the very serious social evils prevalent in the area is Untouchability. The dalits are discriminated in many activities by the non-dalit simply on the basis of caste. Seventy-nine per cent dalit representatives accepted the practice of untouchability in their villages but only 8 non-dalit respondents supported this view. In other words, majority of dalits feel that there is untouchability but majority of the non-dalits feel that there is nothing like untouchability in village locality. However, all those who replied in the affirmative said that mainly social restriction is observed in the case of feeding and drinking.

While 75 per cent dalits feel that there is no effort on the part of panchayat to eliminate this problem, 29 per cent non-dalits shared this view. In other words, more than 50 per cent non-dalits feel that since there is nothing like untouchability therefore question of effort to deal with this problem does not arise. One of the dalit respondents even said that since untouchability is a part of our tradition, therefore, there is no possibility to deal with this problem. Two dalits said that a couple of months back a joint feeding programme was organized in collaboration with pan-chayat, but it did not continue in the coming days. Fourteen per cent non-dalit and 4 per cent dalit respondents said that awareness generation programme are organized to deal with this problem, but these programmes are constantly not organized.

Besides untouchability, there are some other problems specifically found among dalits. For example, 18 and 21 per cent dalit and non-dalit respondents feel that alcoholism is very popular among them. All the major problems created by alcoholism is also faced by dalits of these villages. Besides this, the problem of internal infighting and lack of employment opportunity are also experienced by them. Therefore, a significant number of dalit and non-dalit representatives feel that the dalits should be prohibited to take liquor. For this, on constant basis, anti-liquor programme should be organized. Four respondents observe that by giving reservation to the dalit workers at the local level government induced employment opportunity, their problems may be reduced if not eradicated.

Panchayat Election and its Impact

Respondents have experienced both gains and pains from panchayat. But the gains are only with few respondents in the direct sense, and there are many who have experienced difficulties. In terms of gain some respondents feel that there is change in their mind-set and level of awareness in the positive direction. One of the dalit respondents also received piece of land because of his formal association with panchayat, but there are many who have faced other problems. For instance, 29 per cent dalits had to suffer economic loss because of panchayat work, 3 dalits had to suffer prestige loss, one family went under debt and 2 had to face difficulties in day-to-day life. Hence, while one dalit had gain there are 14 dalits who had to experience pain due to the panchayat assignment. It is needless to mention that there are 8 dalit respondents who are mainly agricultural workers and another 8 are both agriculturists and wage earners. In contrary to this, only 5 non-dalits have to go through these difficulties. Hence, while 50 per cent dalits had no problem from the panchayat work, 62 per cent non-dalits fall under this response category. This is clear from Table 3.14.

Table 3.14 : Economic loss of the respondents in terms of their annual income

Annual Income	Income Loss	
	Dalit	Non-dalit
Upto Rs. 5000	1	1
5000 – 10000	14	2
10000 – 20000	1	2
20000+	2	6
Total	18	11

Opinions about next Election

Since there are many representatives from both the social categories who are facing difficulties due to panchayat work, therefore, 50 per cent dalits and 46 per cent non-dalits have decided that they will not contest the next panchayat election. They feel that since they are not effective and powerful in dealing with panchayat work and extending benefit to the villagers, therefore, it is immoral to represent them without doing anything. Also, the dalits are not in a position to suffer economic loss on constant basis. Some of the specific reasons responsible for discouraging the representatives to contest the next election are voicelessness on their part, ineffectiveness, status degradation, lack of cooperation from officials, personal loss, criticism by people, lack of gain, and desire of the relatives to contest the election. The finding reveals that no gain/personal loss is the main reason discouraging non-dalit representatives to contest the next election. But in the case of dalits voicelessness, status degradation and no gain are the main inhibiting factors. This is clear from following Table 3.15.

Table 3.15 : Reasons for not contesting next election

Reasons	Dalit			Non-dalit		
	Sarpanch	Panch	JP Member	Sarpanch	Panch	JP Member
No voice	–	3	–	–	3	–
Relatives will contest	–	2	–	–	–	–
Status degradation	3	1	–	–	–	–
Officials non-cooperative	–	–	1	–	–	–
No gain	2	–	–	–	–	1
Criticism	–	–	–	–	1	–
Personal loss	–	–	–	2	3	–
Total	5	6	1	2	7	1

But about 39 per cent respondents from both the categories will contest the next election. They will contest the election under various conditions and for various reasons. For example, 2

Panches will contest for the post of Sarpanch, because nobody listens to panch, 11 per cent dalit and 14 per cent non-dalit respondents said that in order to complete successfully the ongoing development programmes under their leadership they will contest the next election. Few of the respondents feel that if the reservation facility is again available to them they will contest the election. One dalit and 2 non-dalits will surely contest the election for their own vested political interest. 4 respondents said that as yet it is undecided but in case they are approached by the villagers they will definitely contest the election particularly for the empowerment of dalits.

Interpersonal Relations

Both the dalit and the non-dalit respondents have to work with the non-dalit and the dalit co-representatives, local influentials government officials and others. Cordial relations for the cause of proper functioning is essential. In course of the study it was observed that 21 dalits and 15 non-dalits had good relationship with the dalit representatives. In the remaining cases the relationship was neither good nor bad. But in contrary to this 3 dalit and 1 non-dalit representatives had bad relationship with the panchayat level non-dalit representatives. One of the woman dalit respondents said that she had hostile relationship because they brought no-confidence motion against her.

Similarly at the JP level the nature of relationship between the dalit and the non-dalit members and *vice versa* is neither good nor bad. Actually there is no legal linkage between panches and the JP level representatives. So far as relationship between the gram panchayat level representatives and the district level members is concerned, in the case of both the nature of relationship is indifferent because they are officially not related to each other.

But the relationship between the *Gram Panchayat* representative and the panchayat secretary is very frequent and therefore, there is total lack of indifferent relation between these two. But by and large in case of more than 50 per cent respondents their relation with panchayat secretary is good. There are, however, 21 per cent dalit and 11 per cent non-dalit representatives whose relation with panchayat secretary is bad. This is primarily because the secretary do not listen to them and in some of the cases the panchayat representatives are cheated by these secretaries. In certain cases these secretaries are government staff but in another case they are appointed by sarpanch mainly on the basis of primordial considerations. The relations with government officials and political worker is by and large good. But at the local level there are cases of tense relation particularly with the local level influentials and the dalit representatives.

Overcoming Problems of Dalit Representatives

On the basis of above analysis it is clear that there are some of the specific problems of dalit representatives and some problems are of general nature. It is essential that in order to strengthen these representatives, efforts should be made to deal with both the specific and the general problems separately. For this purpose both the dalit and the non-dalit respondents have given their suggestions. Important among these are the following: 36 per cent dalits said that their problem should be heard by all the concerned honestly before making effort to solve it, 11 per cent said that without educating dalits in general and dalit representatives in particular their problems cannot be solved. Batanlal, a dalit Panch of Bichia Panchayat suggested that "General caste people do not allow us to speak. If I will speak I will invite trouble for me. Nobody listens to me because I am dalit. Government should again and again say the non-dalits to listen to our voice." Some respondents said that JP members should come forward to solve their problems. Two respondents are of the view that land/work opportunity should be provided to dalits as such on priority basis. They are of the opinion that in order to strengthen the dalit representatives it is essential that the dalit masses should be empowered. In this connection Dwarka Singh, a dalit Panch of Thuna Kala Panchayat said that "Near the forest area 750-800 acres of land are lying vacant. All the landless dalits of my Panchayat should be allotted upto 2.5 acres of land out of this lying land." Suggestions pertaining to the solution of the problems of dalit representatives and their empowerment are presented through the following Table 3.16.

Table 3.16 : Overcoming Problems of Dalit Representatives

S. No	Response	Dalit		Non-Dalit	
		Frequency	Per cent	Frequency	Per cent
1	No resnonse/no reply	1	4	10	36
2	Problems must be heard	10	36	5	18
3	JP should solve problem	2	7	–	–
4	Sarpanch should cooperate	1	4	–	–
5	BPL list should be prepared honestly	2	7	–	–
6	People should be educated	3	11	5	18
7	No difficulties faced	2	–	3	11
8	Govt. should solve it	–	–	2	7
9	Mutual help can solve	–	–	1	4
10	Dalit's work should be solved on priority basis	–	–	1	4
11	Land/work opportunity should be provided	2	7	–	–
12	2+3+4	3	11	–	–
	Total	28	100	28	100

Significant number of non-dalit respondents (36%) did not respond to this question but 5 of them are of the view that the problem of the dalit representatives should be carefully heard, education should be popularized among them and all this work should be done by the government through people's cooperation.

Reservation Facility

Majority of the dalit representatives (71%) feel that reservation facility in itself is not sufficient for the empowerment of dalit representatives in particular and dalit masses in general. It opens door only for the limited people and that too to a limited extent. In contrary to this 43 per cent non-dalits said that it is a sufficient condition for the overall empowerment of the dalit community. But only 14 per cent dalit representatives replied in the same fashion. In other words, there are 16 representatives, i.e. 4 dalits and 12 non-dalits who perceive reservation facility as a sufficient condition for the development of dalits. It is beneficial because it helps them to get chair and because of that position the door of development is opened in different walks of life.

One of the dalit respondents said that if the government. is really interested to empower dalit masses, the upper limit of reservation facility should further be increased.

Those who feel that reservation facility is not sufficient, they also provide different reasons to support their point. They say that reservation without education, awareness, more and more legal rights, employment opportunity, lack of strong voice, honesty etc. is meaningless. They say that besides reservation they must have various types of resources then only reservation facility can really empower the dalit representatives and the masses. If the existing change agents are corrupted and deresponsibilised and in case these change agents are biased, positive reference group for the dalit elites who are still in making, in that situation like other agents the dalit leaders will also remain ineffective for the development of the dalit masses. Therefore, it is essential that along with reservation facility other support system should be made available to all the concerned at the community level.

NGO and Dalits' Development

Conceptually there is direct relationship between NGO and dalits empowerment particularly in the remote rural and tribal areas. This is because NGO live with them, understand them and their problem informally and try to solve it with the active cooperation of dalits. It is needless to mention that there are some NGOs working in the area under study. *Samarthan* is one among them. One of its objectives in the area is to strengthen participatory development process through PRI related organizations. More specifically, from this point of view it has two specific objectives on which it is concentrating since last few years. These are the following :

- Enhancing the participation of the SCs/STs and women in the process of decentralization with informed decision-making capacities.
- Establishing examples of democratic decentralization in the state of Madhya Pradesh.

For meeting the above objectives, Samarthan Sehore is working intensively in 127 panchayats in Sehore Block and it is indulged with these activities since its inception. Some of the specific works done by this organization are the following

- Greater emphasis on training at the village level rather than block level.
- Initiatives were taken by the Panch/Sarpanch Network to organize the training in 120 Panchayats.
- Combined meetings of Mahila Mandals and Gram Sabha committees organized to facilitate interaction between the men and women.
- Intensive trainings at the village level with the involvement of youths belonging to the respective villages. This is ensured a better response to the capacity building initiatives.
- Initiatives to organize *mohalla* level meeting before the Gram Sabha to ensure quality discussion during the Gram Sabha and also to fulfil the required quorum of 20 per cent.
- Mobilization through door-to-door campaign to inform people about the importance of Gram Sabha. This was done in the Khandwa village.
- Prior information about the date/time and venue was given to the Gram Sabha members in 30 villages.
- Rallies of school children were organized prior to the Gram Sabha in 120 villages.
- Use of devotional songs and other forms of folklore and superimposing the need to participate in Gram Sabha in 30 villages.
- Natak (street plays) were organized in Sehore to spread the message of participation in Gram Sabha.
- We organized an exhibition in which posters on Gram Swaraj were displayed. This invoked interest among the villagers and as a result 1500 copies of the booklet on Gram Swarajya were sold.
- Participation in the NSS camps for orientation of the students on PRI issues.
- Micro-planning was used as a tool for Gram Sabha mobilization. Micro-planning helps in restoring the faith of Gram Sabha members and is as effective method of

mobilizing the Gram Sabha members. Micro planning was organized in 46 villages.

- The formation of women SHGs in 20 villages was instrumental in increasing women's participation.
- Developing micro-plans in 46 Panchayats with the major focus on drought.
- Ad hoc Committees were created and delegated the responsibility of micro-planning.
- Possibility of external sources of funds were explored.
- Use of community contributions and panchayat funds was also made.
- Amongst the micro plans made, 49 per cent of the resources were provided by the Panchayat, 26 per cent by the community in form of *Shramdaan* (labour) and the rest 25 per cent was provided by the various organizations involved.
- In 40 villages efforts are being made to make comprehensive plans which are in turn being included with the Annual Plan of the respective villages.
- Documentation of experiences on micro-planning based on the experiences of micro-planning was done by the respective organization.
- Support to Dalit/Women Panchayats is mainly facilitated through the Network of Panchayat Representatives being formed in 46 Panchayats.
- One to one contact was established with the women and Dalit Representatives.
- Advocating the issues of women and Dalit Representatives in various forums.
- Need for making separate network of women elected representatives has been voiced and felt by them.
- Cluster level meetings were organized with Women Sarpanches.
- Monthly meetings were organized.
- Preparation of pamphlets, charts, hand bills/posters on Gram Swaraj are widely distributed in the villages.
- The reading material is being prepared in simple/regional languages.

- Periodicals and newsletter covering laws/provisions, case studies have been made in simplified languages and are being circulated in the panchayat and the village level.
- Mahila Sangathana was formed comprising Anganwadi workers for information dissemination.
- Selling of the *Pothi Gram Swaraj ki* at the Gram Sabha level.
- Audio cassette "Bundeli Geeton mein Gram Swaraj" has been prepared in four volumes and till now 940 sets of the cassette have been distributed.
- Publishing the newsletter called *Gaon ki Chithi* are widely disseminated. Now there are 400 annual members for the same.

There are some NGOs working in the study area but majority of the respondents, i.e. 68 per cent dalits and 61 per cent non-dalits feel that its role for dalit and area development is not strongly visible. The NGOs are either ineffective or they are not in contact with the poor dalit or non-dalit masses. But there are 6 respondents who said that in their area the NGOs have constructed latrine and it has launched literacy programme. Some of the respondents also reported that they have constructed bridge, latrine in schools, organized training programme, constructed school building and provided drainage facility. But critically speaking it is bit difficult to say that how these works are directly related to development of the dalit community. Similarly majority of the works done by the NGOs except *Samarthan*, are related to construction. They have still to attack those aspects and issues which create problem for social and cultural development. Hence, critically speaking there is no fundamental difference between the work of panchayat and the work of NGOs because both of them mainly concentrate on construction work rather for social and economic development of the people. Therefore, respondents have made some suggestions for the NGO from the point of view of empowerment of the dalit representatives in particular and the dalit masses in general. Some of the specific suggestions are clear from the following Table 3.17.

Table 3.17 : NGO and development of dalits

S. No	Response	Dalit		Non-Dalit	
		Frequency	Per cent	Frequency	Per cent
1	No response	3	11	7	25
2	Training Programme	–	–	1	4
3	Solve their problem	4	14	4	14
4	Present their demand before the govt.	3	11	1	4
5	Concrete work should be done for them	2	7	4	14
6	Financial help	–	–	1	4
7	Education	3	11	2	7
8	No NGO/no suggestion	1	4	1	4
9	Awareness programme	2	7	5	18
10	2+3+4	6	21	2	7
11	3+4+5	4	14	–	–
	Total	28	100	28	100

On the basis of analysis of Table 3.17, it is clear that hardly a single dalit respondent suggested about the training programme for capacity building of the dalit representatives. Fourteen per cent respondents form both the categories said that their problem should be solved by the government. For this purpose they suggested that besides doing at its own the NGO should represent their problem before the government. Majority of the respondents still perceive government as the most powerful institution to solve their problems. They have still to realize the role of Panchayat and the NGO in this respect. Therefore, they think that both of them should work as the spokesperson of the villagers. However, some respondents said that awareness programme, financial help. education to the illiterate and combination of all these suggestions, if taken into consideration, can definitely help the dalit representatives to participate in the ongoing process of empowerment initiated by the government and civil society bodies.

V

OTHERS PERCEPTIONS

In order to maintain objectivity and transparency in the study, it is essential that opinions of dalit and non-dalit panchayat representatives regarding the functioning and achievement of panchayat under their leadership must be verified from different sources. In this context it is essential that views of some of the members of *gram sabha* and local level government officials associated with Panchayat activities should be collected. If the views of panchayat representatives are broadly similar to the views of the above mentioned respondents, it can be inferred that the responses provided by the representatives are closer to the reality. For this purpose we interviewed cross-section of population. Their views are analyzed and presented in the following manner.

Views of Gram Sabha Members

We interviewed 12 Gram Sabha members, i.e. 6 dalits and 6 non-dalits and from these we interviewed 6 men and 6 women. Majority of them (9) are illiterate and from above 35 years of age. All of them are by and large engaged in agriculture work but 4 of them are specifically wage earners, 8 respondents have land and 4 are landless. So far as views about performance of Sarpanch is concerned, 58 per cent feel that they are not doing well. They reasoned that the sarpanch is doing favour to his own people. Because of politics the functions of *Sarpanch* is negatively affected. One of the respondents Laxmi Narayan (OBC) said that "The sarpanch cannot do any of his work in the concrete sense. The ex-sarpanch was committed to do development work and he increased income of the panchayat. Actually he constructed shops and connecting roads, but the present sarpanch is unable to do anything. He has no capacity." Similarly Dhankuwar Bai said that "The ex-sarpanch was very dynamic but he used to do work as per his own liking and disliking. He was not dictated by anybody." But an illiterate Gendalal (SC) said about the functioning of non-SC sarpanch in the following manner. "Neither the ex-sarpanch nor the current sarpanch is sensitive to the problem of the people. In my house there is neither electricity nor drinking water facility. In spite of my meeting with the sarpanch they (both ex and the present) have been failed to provide me the above facilities." But Tulsi Bai (SC) said that the current sarpanch and his functioning is not inferior to that of the previous sarpanch. Actually he did lot of development work for the entire village. Similarly Keshar Bai said that both the present sarpanch and ex-sarpanch are good, but the present sarpanch is better than the ex-sarpanch because he is more committed to the cause of village. Within last few months he constructed connecting road and small bridge in the village.

In response to a question about the performance of panchayats representatives both the dalit and the non-dalit villagers said that they have constructed road, school building, hand-pump, houses, bridge, well repair and latrine in school. Non-dalit villagers also said that extension of school building and boundary wall was made. But, whether these achievements are sufficient or not, maximum number of them, i.e. 8 out of 12 said that it is not because some other important work like land to the landless, house to the houseless, PDS facility, employment opportunity and health care facility is required, but the representatives have done no concrete effort in this direction.

Do the dalit representatives promote harmony among the castes? about half of the respondents replied in the positive. They said that partly they have contributed to frequent and positive interaction between the castes, but partly it has benefited only the dalit representatives. Dalit representatives behave like monarch in their group, feel respected and they have contributed to improvement in the social reputation of a section of dalits, who are related to them. The common dalits have gained nothing from the dalit representatives. Actually these representatives are failed to deal with caste based discrimination due to fear of vote and no confidence motion. This view was expressed by all the dalit respondents.

Gram Sabha Meeting

So far as presence and participation of villagers in gram sabha meeting is concerned only 2 dalit and 2 non-dalit respondents attend it. They attend it in order to discuss village problem, get information about development work and to pass the resolution so that it may be send to the JP panchayat. About 67 per cent respondents do not attend the meeting because they do not get benefit, do not receive information in time, they cannot leave the wage work, dalits are not properly invited and there is quarrel in the meeting. However, in order to ensure success of *Gram Sabha* meeting they have given some suggestions and the dalits are more serious and active while giving the suggestions. These suggestions are: if work is done honestly with the help of people, *gram sabha* is directly involved in the development work, no politics is done and *gram sabha* committees are honestly formed, the success of *gram sabha* can be ensured. However, 2 of the non-dalit respondents said that reservation facility should be removed to secure its functioning.

In many cases sarpanch has to do work under pressure. 5 dalits and 2 non-dalits expressed this view. They said that because of favouritism, corruption and manipulation the sarpanch looses their integrity and therefore, they have to do work under pressure, but if they take help from all and if people are divided on caste line the amount of pressure is countered by another pressure.

Peoples Expectation from Panchayat

The finding reveals that non-dalits have more expectation than the dalit villagers from their representatives. However, from both the categories, respondents have more than one expectation. Some of the salient expectations are the following. They want village bridge, inclusion of their name in the BPL list, water, road and housing problem to be solved, land to the landless, social justice, employment opportunity and solution of drainage, health, latrine and solution of electricity problem. A couple of respondents feel that the problem of school, stop dam etc., should also be solved by these representatives. This is clear from Table 3.18.

In order to ensure smooth functioning of panchayat it is needed that panchayat representatives should be strengthened and empowered by all the concerned. For this purpose respondents have given some suggestions. Some of the specific suggestions are: if government grant is increased and released timely, panchayat representatives are encouraged to attend more and more training programmes, they do work honestly and boldly, people participate with them and development oriented work is done on priority basis, the representatives will feel more and more empowered because the villagers will honestly support them.

Table 3.18 : Villagers expectation from Panchayat Representatives

Response	Dalit		Non-dalit	
	Frequency	Per cent	Frequency	Per cent
13+14	1	17	–	–
2+7	1	17	–	–
3+11+12	1	17	–	–
8+10	1	17	–	–
1+7+8+17	1	17	–	–
4+6+7	1	17	–	–
14+17	–	–	1	17
5+12+15+16	–	–	1	17
1+5+9+13	–	–	1	17
4+5	–	–	1	17
1+6	–	–	1	17
1+4+5+6	–	–	1	17
Total	6	100	6	100

Note : (1) Village Bridge. (2) Only rich are benefited. (3) Name inclusion in BPL list. (4) Water problem. (5) Road Problem. (6) Housing problem. (7) Wage opportunity. (8) Possession of land. (9) Justice. (10) Solution of drainage problem. (11) Health facility. (12) Electricity. (13) Latrine facility. (14) Total development of village. (15) School facility. (16) Stop dam facility. (17) Honest behaviour of repesentative.

Role of Secretary

In this context the villagers criticized the role played by the panchayat secretary. It is needless to mention that out of 12 villagers, 11 see negative points with the secretary. They feel that panchayat secretary is not cooperative. He only attend the meeting and do not do the work. Two respondents feel that he is corrupted, manipulative and rarely visit the village. One respondent said that he has manipulated the old age persion fund. One non-dalit villager feels that secretary of his panchayat work under pressure of sarpanch. He does not listen to the poor villagers. Hence, most of the community members, irrespective of their caste background, are critical to the functioning of panchayat secretary.

Major Problems in Panchayat

Sehore is one of the underdeveloped *tehsils* of M.P. in terms of most of the indicators of development. It is full of problem. But perception about problem slightly differ from person to person depending upon their social base. In response to a question about any three problems observed by the respondents, it was found that of 12 villagers, 11 villagers have perceived problems. Some of them perceived even more than three problems. These problems are the following: the problem of water, road, electricity, drainage, health, toilet etc. It was perceived by significant number of respondents. Some feel lack of toilet, school, tank etc. as the main problem. There is encroachment of road which create problem for a couple of respondents. Similarly land dispute is also serious. This is clear from the following Table 3.19.

Table 3.19 : Major Problems of the villages as perceived by villagers

Response	Dalit		Non-dalit	
	Freauency	Per cent	Frequency	Per cent
1+4+10+11	1	17	–	–
8+11+12	1	17	–	–
5+7+8	1	17	–	–
1+2+4+6	1	17	–	–
1+4	1	17	–	–
1+9	1	17	–	–
1+13	–	–	1	17
11+12	–	–	1	17
1+4+5	–	–	1	17
1+2	–	–	1	17
1+3+4	–	–	1	17
1+2+3	–	–	1	17
Total	6	100	6	100

Note :(1) Water problem, (2) Road problem, (3) Electricity problem, (4) Drainage problem, (5) Lack of health facility, (6) Lack of toilet facility, (7) Lack of veterinary hospital, (8) Conflict related to land, (9) No pension to widow/handicapped, (10) Lack of proper cost of crop, (11) Lack of school, (12) Encroachment of road.

Dalit Empowerment

Do the reservation facility has empowered the dalit representatives? All the dalit respondents replied in the negative and half of the non-dalits also replied in the negative. Only 3 non-dalits replied in the affirmative. Those who replied in the negative said that they are not empowered. They are unable to do development work, involved in favouritism and many of the sarpanches are dummy leaders. So far as relationship between dalits' development and NGO is concerned on this issue we received mixed response. While all the dalit respondents and 4 non-dalit respondents said that the role of NGO is insignificant in this context, a couple of non-dalit villagers said that NGO has provided latrine and road facility in the dalit colony. However, the role of panchayat in the development of women and children, is by and large more obvious. About half of the respondents do not see any impact, but half of them feel that it has provided literature through *Anganwadi* worker, medical facility in the locality, midday meal to the poor students, scholarship to children and pension facility to destitutes and dependent women.

On the basis of analysis of views of 12 dalit and non-dalit community members, it is clear that the role of panchayat in village development is relatively more obvious than its role in the empowerment of dalit representatives in particular and the dalit villagers in general. Actually some of the serious problems which are caste based do not draw attention of the panchayat representatives.

Views of Dalit and Non-dalit Government Officials

We interviewed 4 local level government officials to know their views about the functioning of the *Gram Panchayat* from the point of view of Dalit's empowerment. Two were dalit and 2 non-dalit respondents, within it 2 were men and 2 women.

In response to a question about the functioning of GP, one of the non-dalit respondents working in JP office and staying there since last 10 years said, "there is proper understanding between the panchayat representatives. As a result they have done several construction works like the construction of village road, small bridge and repair of Panchayat Bhavan and health centre in a significant manner."

This response was endorsed by another respondent who is woman and staying in Sehore since 1982. But she added that besides the above work many panchayats have successfully prepared BPL list, provided house to the houseless and help to the handicapped. All these works are done by the Panchayat as per the decision of the *Gram Sabha*.

The above observation was partly shared by 2 dalit respondents and partly not. Both of them, one male and one female, are living in Sehore since last 5 years. They said that irrespective of caste background if the sarpanch is illiterate and ignorant, the level of performance of the panchayat is poor.

Two of the respondents are satisfied with the functioning of Panchayat and 2 not. Those who are satisfied (both dalit and non-dalit) said that since the target related to construction/social security work is timely completed, therefore it seems that the panchayats are doing well. However, the dalit respondent (CEO) said that since he has not received any complaint about the malfunctioning of panchayat, since people are now more politically conscious, therefore, it may be said that panchayats are doing well.

Those who replied in the negative said that (a) Panchayat is only doing construction work. It is not doing anything for awareness generation. (b) The area inhabited by the dalits are still waiting for drainage facility.

Dalit Welfare

About the role of Panchayat for dalits' development one of the dalit respondents expressed strong opinion "anti-poverty programme is launched equally for all. Everything is done as per the rule. All the needy, whether dalit and non-dalit, are equally treated." Similar view was expressed by another dalit respondent.

But both of the non-dalit respondents had different story to narrate. They said that special effort was made to provide some facilities like loan, house, connecting road and repair of the community hall located in their area and used by them.

Gram Sabha

Three respondents said that its meeting is organised now twelve times in a year. But one respondent differed. She reasoned that most of the time the quorum is not complete. This is because people have lost faith in the meeting because whatever demand they pass and send to the higher level, most of the time it is not approved. As a result, people think waste of time while attending the meeting.

But those 3 who replied in the affirmative opined that it is organised but to them also people are not enthusiastic to attend the meeting because they do not gain anything quickly. One of the dalit respondents said "Gram Sabha meeting is regularly organised. But in about 40-45 Panchayats (out of 127 Panchayats) the sarpanches motivate only their supporters to attend the meeting in order to conduct the meeting peacefully and successfully. They seldom invite the others."

People's Expectation

What people at large expect from the Gram Panchayat? We received some common and some specific observations. These are mentioned below.

Table 3.20 : Issues in terms of priority

Respondents	
Dalit (Male)	Village development, construction of village road, school building, water facility, name inclusion in BPL list and pension facility.
Dalit (Female)	Facility of water, house, electricity, road and health.
Non-dalit (Male)	Road, Handpump, cleanliness and construction of common facility.
Non-dalit (Female)	The proposal forwarded by the Gram Sabha/Panchayat should be approved and implemented.

Role of Secretary

Secretary is the key institution in the Gram Panchayat. About its functioning respondents expressed mixed views. Dalit respondents expressed critical views and the non-dalit replied in the formal and routinised manner. For instance, the former said that in about 40-45 Panchayats, the Sarpanch is illiterate. In these panchayats the secretaries misuse/exploit the sarpanch. Many of these secretaries do not submit the report in time. People are not happy with many of them. Some of them are corrupted. But the latter said that the Secretaries help the *Sarpanch*, inform the villagers about the schemes and work as link between the Panchayat and the higher level bodies.

Major Problems

Area

The problems of the area are common in nature which is found and experienced in other parts of the region. Respondents have shared common views on this point. The major problems of the area are: lack of connecting road, drinking water, electricity, health facility, education facility, paper related to land ownership, green card, problem related to pension, inclusion of name in BPL list, lack of bridge, lack of assertiveness on the part of villagers in the preparation and sanctioning of budget for rural development, lack of required number of stop dam and lack of tolerance on the part of sarpanch to listen to the problems of villagers.

Dalit

The above mentioned problems are common in nature, therefore, both dalits and non-dalits have to face it. But some problems are dalit specific. For instance, they are the victims of untouchability and alcoholism. The amount of illiteracy and poverty is very serious among them. They also practice child marriage system. Since, they are illiterate, they do not avail benefits of development schemes. Because of alcoholism most of them are engaged in factionalism and infighting. It is surprising to mention that except one occasion, when common feast was organized by ICDS among the dalits and non-dalits in order to reduce untouchability, the efforts are neither made by dalit nor by the non-dalit panchayat representatives to address the above problems.

So far as the role of NGO is concerned, its performance is perceived by the respondents in a mixed manner. For example, the non-dalit respondents highlighted the role of 13 NGOs engaged in watershed programme as well as the role of *Samarthan*, but they did not mention specific role particularly for the solution of the problems of dalit. But they said that *Samarthan* constructed connecting road in the dalit area. Also, it empowered dalits to solve their problems by themselves.

All the four respondents said that the problems of dalits can be addressed properly by the panchayat provided people at large are made conscious, empowered to raise voice and take part in the decision making process. This cannot be done just by educating them. Both the schools/NGOs and panchayats can jointly initiate campaign for this purpose.

VI

CASE STUDY

Re-introduction of Panchayat institution through specific constitutional package, by the government, by introducing 73rd Constitutional amendment is an effort to ensure participation of marginalised groups in the decision making process at the grassroots level. Besides the reservation facility for weaker section, provision of training programme and other interventions have also been made by the state for capacity building of the representatives. Both the dalit and non-dalit representatives have to function in similar socio-political environment, but in spite of that there is difference in their social background, level of awareness and experience in panchayat activities. How, and to what extent the dalit leaders have managed the situation? What are their perception and plan? These are some of the issues which have been comprehended through the case study technique. The cases are mentioned below

1.	Kailash Bai	Non-dalit Woman Sarpanch
2.	Mahesh Kumar Dubey	Non-dalit Sarpanch
3.	Taravati	Dalit Woman Sarpanch
4.	Asharam Bhagat	Dalit Sarpanch

Kailash Bai

Kailash Bai is a *thakur* and woman sarpanch of Dhawala gram panchayat. She lives in a semi-*pucca* house, which lack the basic amenities. She is aged, educated upto primary level, she is housewife with no income of her own. There are 8 members in the family. The main source of livelihood is agricultural activities, because the family own about 40 acres of land of which about half land is irrigated. She has neither connection with any political party, nor she ever participated in any political activity in the past. She feels that today her social status has improved because of her presence in panchyat as a sarpanch.

Economic condition of the family is not very improved although the family is neither under debt nor it has any significant saving. Since, the family is agricultural therefore most of the agricultural instruments are available with it. Also, the family has most of the common household assets with it.

She did not contest the 1994 Panchyat election only because the seat was not reserved for the women. She contested the 1999 election successfully. She feels that the previous Sarpanch did not do much for village development. She has very low level of awareness about social life and she even did not know the margin of her victory and also do not know the reasons of her victory and the reason of defeat of her rival candidate. But, she feels that there is no difference in social status of the candidates who won the 1999 and 1994 election. To her, it is wrong to say that gradually the less powerful representatives are replaced by the more powerful representatives.

She did not receive any training programme. As a result, her level of awareness is still very low. She did not know when the new Panchayati Raj system was introduced. Also, she did not know how much percentage of seats are reserved for dalits and women in the panchayat. Also, she did not know about the rights and duties of panchayat representatives. But she knows that logic behind introducing Panchayati Raj was to make the villagers self-reliant. This information she got while attending the panchayat meeting. She also said that she did not receive any specific cooperation from anybody. Also, no pressure is experienced on her from any corner. She said that panchayat is doing work as per the decision taken in the *gram sabha* meeting. Till date she managed to provide village road, handpump, repairing of panchayat bhawan with the help of all, but specifically she has not done work for dalit's empowerment. To her the basic problem faced by dalits in her panchayat is the problem of unemployment/livelihood support, but due to paucity of fund the panchyat is unable to solve this programme.

Untouchability is maintained in the panchyat area. The touchable castes maintain it in feeding and drinking activities and panchayat has done nothing in this regard. As stated earlier, there is improvement in her social status after joining the PRI. She has yet to decide whether she will contest the forthcoming panchayat election or not. So far as relations with the local and the upper level dalit and non-dalit representatives/officials are concerned, in most of the cases, it is friendly. However, her relations with non-dalit representatives of gram panchayat is excellent. Her lack of awareness and assertiveness is also obvious from the fact that she do not have any linkage with government officials, local influentials and the local level political workers.

She feels that by providing education to the dalit children alone their problems may be reduced. To her there is no meaning of reservation facility so long as dalit children do not receive formal education.

Mahesh Kumar Dubey

Mahesh Dubey is an upper caste sarpanch of Raipura *Gram panchayat*. He hails from well-to-do family. The house is *puccka* with most of the households and agricultural assets. The house has separate toilet and drawing room facility. He is about 25 years old. He is professionally trained man, but engaged in farming work. The source of family income is private job and agricultural activities. The family has around 12 acres of irrigated and unirrigated land. He is not under debt, although, the family lack saving.

He is associated with Congress Party since 1990. His father was also associated with the same political party. He has participated in *Dharna*. He is also associated with NGO called *Rastriya Samaj Prakostha Society*. After joining the panchayat there is improvement in his social status.

Dubey did not contest the 1994 election. Actually his application form was rejected for he was under age. He is a conscious representative. He knows that he defeated the nearest rival candidate by 27 votes. To him rival candidate was defeated because of his non-performance. Till date he has attended seven training programmes for 12 days. In the training he learnt about Panchayati Raj and *Gram Swaraj*. He is unable to recall the specific gains from the training programme, but he feels that it has enhanced the level of awareness. This is also clear from the fact that he correctly responded about the year of commencement of new Panchayati Raj, its objectives etc., but at the same time he wrongly mentioned about the exact provision of reservation for dalits and women in PRI. He knows about some of the rights and power of PRI but also feels that it is not sufficient because it do not help representatives to get the work done in time. He feels that as per the Panchayat Act, panchayat must provide house to the houseless, wage to wage earners and also it must constitute small groups for capacity building among the villagers. He learnt about panchayat election from the panchayat office itself. To him if large number of poor are covered under the below poverty line, if development work is organized in a speedy manner and if development schemes are honestly introduced then only society may progress and panchayat may be termed as successful panchayat. With the help of the co-representatives Mahesh Kumar has successfully managed inclusion of names of 25 dalits in the BPL list. 3 people were provided house facility and few of them secured ration card and loan because of his intervention. He do not feel that only reservation facility can uplift the status of dalits. He said that so long as separate residential colonies are not constructed for dalits, fruit of development schemes are not ensured for them, land is not given to the landless, light, road and drinking water facility is not provided and pressure is not created for removal of untouchability, the condition of dalits cannot improve. This dream can only be materialized provided there is proper cooperation among *gram sabha*, higher level panchayats, bank and the district level bureaucracy. He perceived that there are three basic problems in his panchayat which is experienced by all. These are related to village road, electricity and drinking water. Dubey will fight the forthcoming election for the post of Janpad member. He has friendly relations with the panchayat representatives of all the three levels as well as the government officials. He suggests that development of dalits is only possible provided government support is made available to them in time. Educational development can facilitate development in other walks of life. He cited the role of *Samarthan* in the construction of village road and drainage system. But he suggested that such activities should be done on constant basis.

Taravati

Taravati is a dalit woman sarpanch of Doraha Gram Panchayat. She is relatively well-to-do because besides other facility, she has the facility of telephone, independent drawing room etc. She has also cooler, radio and television facility and a two-wheeler. She herself is educated upto middle level and the family has income of more than Rs. 20000 per annum. Hence, she is a dalit representative but, the family fall under middle income group. Including her, there are 4 persons in the family. She and her husband are construction worker. The family is under debt. Few years back she took loan of more than Rs. 5000 from a local *Sahukar* for social activities.

She is a member of Congress Party since long. Her husband is also the supporter of Congress Party, although none of them have ever participated in political activism.

She has gained nothing, even in terms of social status, from the panchayat. Rather, she and her husband have to suffer wage work because of involvement in panchayat activities.

She did not contest the first election of panchayat because, at that time the Sarpanch post was not reserved for dalit woman. Hence, reservation facility directly benefited her and she became sarpanch. She admitted that she did not receive any grant from any source, but in spite of that she has constructed village road and drainage system with people's participation. She is a popular and enlightened person. This is clear from the fact that she defeated the nearest rival candidate by the margin of 147 votes. This is also clear from the fact that she gave proper response to the question related to reservation for dalits in panchayat. She attended a training programme organized by *Samarthan* for three days and received information about different schemes. She knows when the new Panchayati Raj was introduced but she do not know the specific reason behind it. She do not know about provisions in panchayat manual for women's development. She feels that there are rules and provisions, but its benefits are not provided to the poor dalits. Only rich people manage the benefits. She knows that her main work is to look after the village, solve the villagers problem and instruct the officials. She received information about the rights and duties of panchayat representatives from the primary sources. One of the specific problems in the way of development of dalits are lack of approval of the projects submitted by her in time because the previous sarpanch committed manipulation and inquiry is pending against him. In order to get approval she wrote letters to the administration as well as published the difficulties in the newspaper, but in spite of that she did not get anything out of this effort. In other words, she do not get any specific help from any source. Occasionally she receives help from the local influentials from the general castes and they do never put any pressure on her. As yet the main work for dalit, which she has done, is the distribution of land among them. In this work she received opposition from a JP member who accused that she wrongfully distributed land among them. She feels that in the future not only more and more number of dalits should be provided land, but also they must have electric connection in their house.

Some of the specific problems faced by the local dalits are related to the practice of untouchability as well as alcoholism among them. She feels that if possible, she will contest for membership in the higher level panchayat. She observes that there are 8 non-dalit representatives in panchayat and they moved no-confidence motion against them, but they did not succeed. The local influentials are not in favour of her because from behind they do not hesitate to criticize her. She concluded that reservation facility is not enough for the empowerment of dalit representatives. Attempt should be made to ensure cooperation from government officials and the local influentials – both elected and reputed – otherwise it would be difficult for person like her, to do something meaningful for the cause of dalits.

Asharam Bhagat

Asharam Bhagat is a sarpanch of Rafikganj Gram Panchayat. He is *Balai* by caste. He belongs to poor family and he is under debt. He has no household and agricultural assets and he possesses hardly 2.5 acres of agricultural land. It is needless to mention that only recently he was provided this land under the scheme of Bhopal Declaration for dalit's empowerment during 2001. Quality of the land is very poor. He has no input to improve the land for agricultural purpose. He is a follower of *Kabir Panth*.

He did not contest 1994 panchayat election. In 1999 election, he defeated the nearest rival by 250 votes. As yet he has attended four training programmes and from these programmes he learnt about *Gram Swaraj* and panchayat. He feels that training programme should be regular to enhance the level of awareness of people. The most serious problem before him is the lack of approval of development schemes from the higher authority. Even his meeting with Minister Incharge did not solve the problem. But in spite of that for the poor dalit he constructed some houses under IAY, connecting roads and prepared some of the defective handpumps. But he feels that in the years to come he will form Self Help Group among dalits and will help them to get loan, so that they can be economically self-reliant. Some of the specific problems of dalits are the problem of employment/wage work, untouchability and landlessness. He will not contest the next election because after becoming sarpanch, he went under debt, as well as the officials and some of the villagers are so individualistic that they do not help him in anyway. He feels that under the given socio-political circumstances empowerment of dalit representatives and the common dalit is not possible. It is possible even in the limited sense provided they are educated and training programme is organized by the government and NGOs on the regular basis.

4

Tribal Leadership in Panchayats

I

METHODOLOGY

Objectives

The study was conducted to achieve the following objectives

- to know social background of tribal leaders at different levels of Panchayat;
- to examine their level of awareness and its sources in relation to their rights and duties as panchayat represen-tatives;
- to discuss the levels of achievements and non-achievements and expectations of panchayat representatives; and
- to find out views of "others" about the functioning of Panchayat under tribal leaders.

Universe

The study was conducted in one of the tribal dominated districts of Madhya Pradesh called "Betul". However, within the district it was conducted in the Betul Development Block. The size of the population in the district is 11,81,501 which reside in 5 *Tehsils* and 10 Development Blocks. Out of 10 Development Blocks there are 7 Tribal Development Blocks (TDB). These are Betul (Population : 1,22,361), Chicholi (56,686), Ghora Dongari (97,573), Shahpur (72,656), Bhains Dehi (84,080), Aathnar (79,132) and Bhimpur (90,092). There are 1,22,361 people living in Betul Block of which 38.36 per cent are tribals. Betul district is geographically spread in 10043 sq. km. There are 1328 villages with having 555 Gram Panchyats. So far as Betul Development Block (BDB) is concerned its geographical area is 1003.92 sq. km, with having 188 villages and 77 Gram Panchayats. Hence, 14.16 and 13.87 per cent of villages and GP of the district are found in the BDB respectively. Further, there are 34 PHCs and 11 Family Welfare Centres in the district of which 7 and 2 PHCs and FWCs are found in Betul Block respectively. Hence, on an average there is one PHC in each of the 94 villages.

The district in general and BDB in particular is electrified because about 95 per cent villages are covered by it. More or less similar is the situation in the case of availability of drinking water facility. There are 2035 primary, 454 secondary, 166 higher secondary and 4 vocational schools in the district respectively. The number of colleges in the district is 7. As per 2001 census report male and female literacy rate in the district is 77.31 and 56.05 (total 66.87) per cent respectively. But in BDB there are 243, 80, 27 and 4 primary, secondary, higher secondary and vocational schools respectively. Also, of 7 colleges in the district, 4 are located in Betul Block itself.

Significant number of PDS are found in both districts (525) and in Betul Block (76). It is found in both rural and urban areas. There are 77 Gram Panchayats in Betul Block. However, all are not headed by tribal sarpanches. Gender, Community/Caste and position-wise distribution of all the three-level panchayat representatives of Betul district as well as Betul Block (as per 1999 election) is presented below.

Table 4.1 : Classification of Z.P. Members on the basis of Caste/Community and Gender (1999)

Block	General		O.B.C.		S.C.		S.T.		Total		Grand Total
	M	F	M	F	M	F	M	F	M	F	
Betul	1	–	–	–	–	–	–	1	1	1	2
Shahpur	–	–	–	–	–	–	1	1	1	1	2
Ghora Dongari	1	–	–	–	1	–	–	–	1	1	2
Chicholi	–	–	–	–	–	–	1	–	1	–	1
Amala	1	–	–	–	–	–	1	–	2	–	2
Multai	–	1	–	1	–	–	–	–	–	2	2
Prabhat Pattan	–	–	1	–	–	1	–	–	1	1	2

(Contd.)

Table 4.1 *(Contd.)*

Bhains Dehi	1	–	–	–	–	–	–	1	1	1	2
Aathner	–	1	–	–	–	–	1	–	1	1	2
Bhimpur	–	–	–	–	–	–	2	–	2	–	2
Total	4	2	1	1	1	1	6	3	11	8	19

Classification of J.P. Members on the basis of Caste/Community and Gender (1999)

Block	General		O.B.C.		S.C.		S.T.		Total		Grand Total
	M	F	M	F	M	F	M	F	M	F	
Betul	4	3	4	2	2	–	6	3	16	8	24
Shahpur	2	2	1	–	1	–	6	4	10	6	16
Ghora Dongari	3	1	2	2	1	–	7	4	13	7	20
Chicholi	2	1	1	–	1	–	4	3	8	4	12
Amala	5	3	4	2	2	1	4	2	15	8	23
Multai	8	4	4	2	1	1	1	1	14	8	22
Prabhat Pattan	5	3	4	2	2	1	3	2	14	8	22
Bhains Dehi	3	2	1	–	1	–	6	4	11	6	17
Aathner	2	2	2	1	1	–	5	3	10	6	16
Bhimpur	1	1	–	–	1	–	10	6	12	7	19
Total	35	22	23	11	13	3	52	32	123	68	191

Classification of Sarpanches on the basis of Caste/Community and Gender (1999)

Block	General		O.B.C.		S.C.		S.T.		Total		Grand Total
	M	F	M	F	M	F	M	F	M	F	
Betul	15	7	13	6	4	3	19	10	51	26	77
Shahpur	–	–	–	–	–	–	26	14	26	14	40
Ghora Dongari	–	–	–	–	–	–	36	19	36	19	55
Chicholi	–	–	–	–	–	–	22	12	22	12	34
Amala	15	8	11	6	7	3	12	6	45	23	68
Multai	24	12	11	6	6	2	5	3	46	23	69
Prabhat Pattan	15	8	11	5	6	4	11	5	43	22	65
Bhains Dehi	–	–	–	–	–	–	32	16	32	16	48
Aathner	–	–	–	–	–	–	30	15	30	15	45
Bhimpur	–	–	–	–	–	–	36	18	36	18	54
Total	69	35	46	23	23	12	229	118	367	188	555

Classification of Panches on the basis of Caste/Community and Gender (1999)

Block	General		O.B.C.		S.C.		S.T.		Total		G. Total
	M	F	M	F	M	F	M	F	M	F	
Betul	282	153	108	54	80	23	294	158	764	388	1152
Shahpur	90	44	–	–	25	24	308	156	423	224	647
Ghora Dongari	119	63	25	13	45	15	399	210	588	301	889
Chicholi	79	41	3	2	20	4	249	125	351	172	523
Amala	273	137	117	66	101	56	202	97	693	356	1049
Multai	397	213	155	77	82	34	67	35	701	359	1060
Prabhat Pattan	268	136	106	52	103	63	180	79	657	330	987
Bhains Dehi	119	62	3	2	44	19	359	184	525	267	792
Aathner	123	57	–	–	46	12	313	155	482	224	706
Bhimpur	64	27	–	–	27	5	503	250	594	282	876
Total	1814	933	517	266	573	255	2874	1449	5778	903	8681

Source : Office of Janpad Panchayat, Betul, June 16, 2002.

On the basis of above presentation it is clear that of 19 Z.P. members 9, i.e. 50 per cent are the tribals. It shows the high level of their participation at the district level panchayat body. At the J.P. level their number is 84 out of total 191 members. Further, there are 555 Sarpanches in the district of which 347 (62.52 %) are the tribals and about 50 per cent of them are the women, which is much above the required 33 per cent seats reserved for them.

In the same way there are 8681 *panches* in the district of which 4323 are the tribals. This clearly reflects that at all the three levels of panchayat, there is numerically dominance of tribals and from within the tribals, the number of women representatives vary from 40 to 50 per cent. This clearly reflects the positive response of the tribals of Betul in favour of the panchayat institution.

There are 1152 *Panches*, 77 *Sarpanches*, 24 J.P. Members and 2 Z.P. members in Betul Development Block. In this block also at all the three levels the number of tribal representatives is much higher in comparison to other social groups. This is clear from the following Table 4.2.

Table 4.2 : Classification of PRI leaders of Betul Block on the basis of status, caste and gender

Position	Total	General			O.B.C.			S.C.			S.T.		
		M	F	T	M	F	T	M	F	T	M	F	T
Panch	1152	282	153	435	108	54	162	80	23	103	294	158	452
Sarpanch	77	14	8	22	13	6	19	5	2	7	19	10	29
J.P.Member	24	5	2	7	4	2	6	1	1	2	6	3	9
Z.P.Member	2	1	–	1	–	–	–	–	–	–	–	1	1
Total	1255	302	163	465	125	62	187	86	26	112	319	172	491

Source : Office of Janpad Panchayat, Betul, June 16, 2002.

Sampling

Altogether 250 respondents of all the three levels of panchayat participated in the study. It is needless to mention that there are 77 Gram Panchayats in Betul Block. The study was conducted in 50 Gram Panchayats. However, from within 50 panchayats only those panchayat representatives were selected for study who were tribals. But *panches* of all the 50 gram panchayats were decided to be interviewed as per their availability during the time of study and we could concentrate on 217 such *panches*. Besides this, the JP president of Betul, 7 JP members of Betul Block and 1 ZP member representing the Betul Block took part in the study (for detail see Table 4.1).

Instrument

The study was conducted with the help of several data collection instruments like secondary source, group interview, case study and semi-structured interview schedule. Semi-structured interview schedule was, however, the main instrument of data collection which was, administered on all the 250 respondents. Interview schedule was broadly divided into 7 heads. Under the opening head caste background and basic information about the family was covered. Under the second heading, social, political and economic points were mentioned. Under the remaining heads questions pertaining to election, training, level and sources of awareness, achievements and expectations, experiences and suggestions for proper functioning of Panchayati Raj institution was covered.

Case study method was used to know, in detail, overall condition of tribal leadership in Panchayati Raj. In order to bring and retain objectivity in the study, views of others such as villagers, government officials etc. were also collected. They concentrated on the current and the emerging interface between tribal leadership and the Panchayati Raj institution.

II

PANCHAYAT REPRESENTATIVES : SOCIAL AND ECONOMIC PROFILE

Betul is a homogeneous development block in terms of its social and demographic conditions and economic life of people. So far as tribals are concerned, like other parts of the district, they are also agriculture/forest based and in modern sense of the term they lack the indices of material development in their life. Although, most of them are from one or two tribes (Gond and Korku) but in terms of occupation, ownership of land, education, possession of household and agricultural assets, as well as availability and use of government induced facilities, they are underdeveloped. Whether, it is the common citizen of the entire Betul Block or its village level panchayat representatives, by and large they all are from the same class and they all are away from the benefits of development process in more or less similar manner. This is clear from the following observations.

Structure of House

In the study 250 respondents participated. Majority of them (241) have *Kaccha* houses. It is made by themselves with the help of locals by locally available raw materials. Even today one can see near absence of modern raw materials in their houses. Not even a single panchayat representative, covered under the study, have *pucca* house.

Position in Panchayat

There are 77 *Gram Panchayats* in Betul Development Block. The study was conducted in 50 *Gram Panchayats.* Since, in each of the studied *Gram panchayat,* tribal *Sarpanches* were not available, therefore, we could interview only 24 *Sarpanches* from 24 *gram panchayats.* But *Panches* of all the 50 *gram panchayats* participated in the study and their number was 217. Also, one *Janpad Panchayat President,* 7 *Janpad Panchayat* members and 1 *Zilla panchayat* member participated in the study. Most of these panchayat representatives were either less educated or illiterate. This is clear from the following Table 4.5. Table 4.3 however provides information about statewise position of our respondents.

Table 4.3 : Classification of Panchayat Representatives who participated in the study

S.No.	Position	Fre.	%
1	Sarpanch	24	9.6
2	Panch	217	86.8
3	Janpad President	1	0.4
4	Janpad Member	7	2.8
5	Zila Panchayat Member	1	0.4
	Total	250	100

Infrastructural Facility

In the entire tribal area of Betul block in particular and among the respondent households in general there is near absence of telephone, handpump/tap water and sanitation facility. For instance, only 9 respondents have telephone and tap water facility. Similarly there are 229 households which do not have sanitation/toilet facility in their own house. They use open space for this purpose. In contrary to this, the availability of electricity and drawing room facility is common among the respondent households. For instance, there are 92.5 per cent and 64.4 per cent households which are electrified and which have drawing room facility respectively. This is clear from Table 4.4.

Table 4.4 : Availability of electricity, telephone, water, sanitation and drawing room facility

	Electricity		Telephone		Hand Pump/Tape Water		Sanitation		Drawing Room	
Response	Yes	No	Yes	No	Yes	No	Yes	No	Yes	No
Frequency	231	19	9	241	9	241	21	229	161	89
%	92.5	7.6	3.6	96.4	3.6	96.4	8.4	91.6	64.4	35.6

Socio-Demographic Profile

Sex

There are 1404 members in all the 250 households. Hence, on an average, there are 5 members in each of the households. But male population slightly outnumber (52.07%) the female population (47.93%). Hence, the sex ratio of Betul is almost similar to the sex ratio existing at the state level.

Age

Family members are from different age groups. But there is one interesting trend which is visible right from the early childhood to the stage of old age, and this trend is from top to bottom. For instance, the number of children is much larger than the number of adult and the number of adult is much larger than the number of senior citizens. Since, the number of senior citizen is only 1.14 per cent, which is much below the state and the national average, therefore, it shows that health status of senior citizen in tribal area is not satisfactory.

Marital Status

The rate of divorce and remarriage of widow/widower is insignificant in the case of respondent households. Also, large number of them (38.46%) are unmarried and 18.23 per cent are minor children. In other words, about 23 per cent members of the respondent households are married. This is clear from Table 4.5.

Education

Educationally Betul district is underdeveloped with only 38.78 per cent and 76.29 per cent literacy rate in rural and urban areas and among the women its percentage is very low, i.e. 56 per cent in comparison to the male literacy rate, i.e. 77 per cent. In case of respondent households about 40 per cent members are illiterate and 5 per cent are minor children. The status of technical and higher education is pitiable among them, because hardly 2 per cent members have received this education.

Occupation

While 12 per cent members are children or physically not fit to work, about 61 per cent members are wage labour. This shows that tribal economy in the area under study is either land based or forest based. Also, significant number of them are engaged in agriculture and labour-cum-agriculture work. The number of members engaged in other occupations like private job, government job, business etc. is less than 7 per cent.

Income

Since, majority of the family members are in wage labour, and large number of the members are dependent, therefore, there are hardly 28 per cent earning hands in the family. Further, out of 28 per cent households, 14 per cent have either or less than the income of Rs. 10000 per annum. There are only 22 households, who have the annual income of either or more than Rs. 20000.

On the basis of the analysis of Table 4.3 it is clear that male outnumber the female population, young outnumber the old population, unmarried outnumber the married population, illiterate or simply literate outnumber the educated population, wage labour outnumber the other occupational groups and poor or household with no source of income outnumber the relatively better income groups. Hence, it is clear that the village level tribal panchayat representatives are from the lower socio-economic status group.

Table 4.5 : Socio-economic status

Sex	Frequency	Percentage
Male	731	52.07
Female	673	47.93
Total	1404	100

Age Group	0-9	10-14	15-24	25-34	35-44	45-59	60+	Total
Freq.	308	287	266	213	224	90	16	1404
%	21.94	20.44	18.95	15.17	15.95	6.41	1.14	100

Marital Status	Not applicable	Unmarried	Married	Divorced	Widow/ Widower	Total
Frequency	256	540	591	5	12	1404
%	18.23	38.46	42.09	0.36	0.85	100

Education	Not applicable	Illiterate	Literate	Primary	Middle	Matric	Technical	UG/PG	Others	Total
Frequency	74	567	209	309	165	59	9	11	1	1404
%	5.27	40.38	14.89	22.01	11.75	4.20	0.64	0.78	0.07	100

Occupation	Not applicable	Labour	Agriculture	Labour+ Agriculture	Private Job	Business	Government Job	Others	Total
Frequency	163	854	105	200	57	9	15	0	1404
%	11.61	60.83	7.48	14.25	4.06	0.64	1.07	0	100

Annual Income (Rs)	Not applicable	Upto 5000	5000-10000	10000-20000	20000+	Total
Frequency	1016	26	173	167	22	1404
%	72.36	1.85	12.32	11.89	1.57	100

Demographic Profile of the Respondents

Tribal leadership in Panchayati Raj is neither dependent on young population below the age of 24 years nor it is in the hands of senior citizen. It is dependent on middle aged population. This is clear from the fact that about 47 per cent of our respondents are between the age group of 35-44 years.

About 95 per cent are married and majority of them (67 per cent) are illiterate or just literate. They are either agriculturist or agriculturist-cum-agricultural workers. Hardly 4 respondents are associated with non-agricultural or allied activities. Since majority of them are in unorganized activity, therefore, level of their annual income is also low. It is needless to mention that about 61 per cent of our respondents are from below the poverty line. But contrary to this there are 8 respondents who have either or more than the income of Rs. 20000 per annum. This is clear from the following Table 4.6

Table 4.6 : Demographic profile of respondents

Age Group	15-24	25-34	35-44	45-59	60+	Total
Freq.	13	72	117	46	2	250
%	5.2	28.8	46.8	18.4	0.8	100

Marital Status	Unmarried	Married	Divorced	Widow/ Widower	Total
Frequency	5	237	3	5	250
%	2	94.8	1.2	2	100

Edu-cation	Illite-rate	Literate	Primary	Middle	Matric	Tech-nical	UG/PG	Total
Freq.	82	85	45	21	13	2	2	250
%	32.8	34	18	8.4	5.2	0.8	0.8	100

Occu-pation	Nothing	Labour	Agri-culture	Labour + Agri-culture	Private Job	Busi-ness	Total
Freq.	76	34	100	36	1	3	250
%	30.4	13.6	40	14.4	0.4	1.2	100

Annual Income (Rs.)	No Income	Upto 5000	5000-10000	10000-20000	20000+	Total
Freq.	76	54	27	85	8	250
%	30.4	21.6	10.8	34	3.2	100

Political Background

In spite of the fact that village level panchayat representatives are from lower socio-economic status, but majority of them (66.4%) are the members of different political parties. They are associated with political parties since long. For example, 14.8 per cent, 28.4 per cent and 26 per cent of the representatives are members of political parties from before 1990, between 1990-95 and since 1995 respectively.

Majority of the respondents (165) are, however, the members or workers of Congress Party. In our study there were only 8 respondents as members or supporters of BJP. In response to a question that do their husband/father have/had political connection with political parties, 169 replied in the affirmative. Here also, 165 said that they were associated with Congress Party. Only 4 were associated with BJP. Eighty-one respondents said that their father/husband had nothing to do with any of the political parties. So far as participation in procession, rally, *dharna,* hunger strike, etc. is concerned, none of the respondents participated in these activities. Similarly only 6 respondents are associated with non-governmental (social and cultural) organisations. It is needless to mention that only 2 NGOs, i.e. RICHA and World Vision, are found in the area under study and only 5 respondents are directly or indirectly associated with these two organisations. As per the perception of these 5 respondents, both these organisations are motivating the tribals to make joint efforts for village development.

Economic Life

Land

Majority of the respondents (205) have land. There are only 16 per cent households who are currently landless. 4 of them had land in the recent past but now they are also landless. So far as amount of land possessed by them is concerned, it is interesting to note that significant number of them (88) have more than 5 acres of land and within it about half of them have even more than 10 acres of land. This shows the nature of relationship between land and the tribal leadership at the village level. In another words, in spite of poor socio-economic condition in terms of education, annual income, occupation and infrastructural facility, most of the tribal representatives are land owners. This is clear from Table 4.7.

Table 4.7 : Land owned by Gram Panchayat Representatives

S. No.	Response	Frequency	%
1	Landless	39	15.6
2	Upto 2.5 Acres	46	18.4
3	2.5-5 Acres	77	30.8
4	5-10 Acres	48	19.2
5	10+ Acres	40	16
	Total	250	100

Now the question is, why in spite of availability of sufficient amount of land, majority of the respondents households are poor? This is perhaps because of poor quality of available land and unavailability of other necessary inputs like irrigation, technical knowledge, HYV seeds, market capital and such other inputs in sufficient manner. Hence, due to absence of all these inputs they are forced to remain poor in spite of availability of huge amount of land.

This observation is supported by the fact that 134 households (54%) do not have any irrigation facility, 30 have 100 per cent land under irrigation and the source of irrigation is duck well, tube well, river and combination of any of the two. 28, 7 and 17 respondents have 50 per cent, 25 per cent and less than 25 per cent of their land under irrigation. However, in the case of only few respondents irrigation facility is available for the entire year. This fact supports the above argument that land without irrigation is not beneficial in the case of 53.6 per cent respondents.

Loan and Saving

Problem of indebtedness is serious among the village level panchayat representatives. Seventy-nine of them are under debt. Fifty-one have taken loan of either or more than Rs. 5000 each. They took loan for various purposes. However, majority of the loanees (68) have taken loan from local bank and cooperative societies. The remaining received loan from the informal sources, viz., friends, relatives and neighbours. Also, of the 79 loanees, majority of them (52) have taken loan for agricultural purpose. None of them took loan for litigation/treatment. Only 8 took loan for consumption/marriage purpose.

Panchayat representatives have also saving. Only 92 of them do not have saving. Many of them are already under debt. The remaining respondents have the saving of between Rs. 1000 to Rs. 5000 and above.

Agricultural/ Household Assets

Respondents are from agricultural background but many of them still possess the traditional means of production. For instance, plough, bullock cart and ox is possessed by 79, 76 and 78 per cent households respectively. In contrary to this, tractor, thresher, harvester and sprayer is possessed by 2, 3 and 0 per cent respondents respectively. However, there are 27 per cent respondents who possess pump set. On this basis it may be said that technological modernization in agriculture is yet to take place even among the Gram Panchayat level tribal representatives.

Table 4.8 : Agricultural/ Household Assets

Agri-cul-tural	Plough		Bullock Cart		Tractor		Thres-her		Ox		Harves-ter		Sprayer		Pump set	
Res.	Y	N	Y	N	Y	N	Y	N	Y	N	Y	N	Y	N	Y	N
Freq	197	53	189	61	5	245	7	243	195	55	0	250	4	246	67	183
%	79	21	76	24	2	98	3	97	78	22	0	100	2	98	27	73

House-hold	Cooler/ Fan		Bicycle		Scooter/ Motor-Cycle		Car/Jeep		Radio/ Tape		TV/ VCR	
Res.	Y	N	Y	N	Y	N	Y	N	Y	N	Y	N
Frequency	66	184	164	86	21	229	1	249	87	163	24	226
%	26	74	66	34	8	92	0.4	99.6	35	65	10	90

Note : Y–Yes, N–No.

So far as household assets are concerned, here also, except bicycle, majority of the households do not possess modern assets. For example, fan/cooler is only available with 26 per cent households although 92.5 per cent have electric connection in their houses. Further, scooter and car/jeep is available with 8 and 0.4 per cent households respectively. Radio/Tape recorder is more popular in comparison to TV /VCR because former is available with 35 per cent and the latter is available with only 10 per cent households. Bicycle is available with 66 per cent households. Actually it is the main source of transportation for tribals most of whom live in the remote rural areas. This is clear from Table 4.8.

On the basis of above analysis it is clear that tribal leadership in Panchayati Raj institution in tribal dominated district like Betul is under the leadership of tribals representing the lower socio-economic status. They have electricity facility, drawing room facility but they do not have the facility of drinking water and sanitation at their own level. Majority of the panchayat representatives are associated with Congress Party since long. The problem of indebtedness is serious among them but majority of the loanees have taken loan from the secondary sources not for consumption but for agricultural purpose. In an earlier study in a tribal dominated district like Jhabua many scholars have observed that most of the tribals under debt have taken loan for consumption purpose. In spite of the ongoing process of modernization among the tribal representatives there in near absence of modern household assets among them but in the case of agricultural assets also modernization process is yet to get momentum. This is clear from the fact that 195 households have ox but tractor is available with only 5 respondents. Not even a single respondent have harvester of their own.

III

LEVEL OF AWARENESS

Awareness on the part of users or beneficiaries, interventionist or change agent is one of the pre-conditions for success of development projects. Importance of awareness further increases in case the procedure of the governance is democratic and success dependent on the participation of development beneficiaries at different levels. In the case of Panchayat representatives it is necessary for them to know their rights and duties, role of government and different schemes formulated and implemented by them. Importance of awareness further increases if the social and political environment is yet to become democratic even after decades of freedom and the representatives are illiterate and their level of social development is low. This section deals with different aspects of awareness available with the Panchayat representative as well as their access to different sources of awareness.

Introduction of Panchayati Raj

Many of our respondents (24.8%) are panchayat representatives since 1994, but significant number of them do not know when the new Panchayat Raj institution was introduced. For instance, while 22.4 per cent respondents did not respond to this question, 24 per cent replied in the negative. Roughly 54 per cent respondents know that it was introduced in 1994. However, none of them know the correct month and date when the PRI was introduced by the Government. of Madhya Pradesh.

Why new Panchayati Raj system was introduced? 32.4 per cent respondents do not know its objective, but 24.4, 9.6 and 10.4 per cent respondents said that, it was introduced for village development, for benefit to poor and for establishing direct linkage between development benefit and the villagers respectively. Further, some of the respondents also observed that it was introduced in order to solve the problem of village level unemployment, underpayment, housing, water and roads. Some respondents (7) feel that objective behind introduction of Panchayati-Raj was primarily to enhance level of awareness of people about their constitutional rights and social responsibilities. Majority of the respondents (60%) know that there is 33 per cent reservation for women in the PRI but none of them actually know the reasons of this facility.

Problems of Villagers

Although study was conducted in relatively homogeneous socio-economic environment, however, panchayat representatives perceive problems in their respective areas in different manner. About 32 per cent respondents do not see problem in their villages, 16.8 per cent feel that water problem is very serious in their villages. Similar number of respondents said that both the problems of village road and water is equally problematic in their constituency. Some respondents (3.2%) said that while preparing the list of population from below poverty line (BPL list) many genuine persons were left out. It created doubt on the integrity of the agency who prepared the list. Some respondents also feel that problem of health facility, transportation, drainage, housing and education needs to be addressed by the panchayat in support of the government. There are some respondents who perceive visibility of more than one problem in the village. They also observe that many of the problems are inter related.

In response to the question that how panchayat representatives come to know about the problem of the villagers, 39.6 per cent said that it is the villagers, who individually or collectively inform them about people's problem. 26.8 per cent respondents themselves observe problem because they themselves live in the villages. On this basis, it is clear that it is the informal source of information which intimate the panchayat representative about the village level problems. 30.4 per cent respondents do not see any problem in their villages. This may be because either their perception of problem is different or the nature of problem is not very alarming in their area.

Rights and Duties

Maximum number of respondents (124) do not know their rights as a panchayat representative. They do not know the efforts and action which they are entitled to undertake in different conditions. Thirty-four did not respond to this question and the remaining 36.8 per cent claim that they know their legal rights. Most of those who said that they know their rights, also perceive that it is sufficient. Only few (11) feel that it is not sufficient to exercise their power. Few of them (9) said that representatives are either unable to exercise their authority primarily because they do not know their rights and some said that it is the subjective decision of *panch* and *sarpanch* which actually defeat the purpose of Panchayati-Raj and therefore, they suggest that effort should be made to motivate them to take decision in objective and value free manner.

So far as duties of panchayat representative is concerned, 41.6 per cent clearly said that the representative should do needful for the total development of the villagers. 8.8 per cent feel that it is the duty of panchayat representative to solve various complaints received by the panchayat. About 43 per cent do not have any knowledge about the duties of panchayat representatives. This is clear from Table 4.9.

Table 4.9 : Commitment towards villagers' problems

S. No.	Response	Frequency	%
1	No knowledge	108	43.2
2	Literacy campaign	0	0
3	Cleanliness of village	1	0.4
4	Provide drinking water	1	0.4
5	Solve complain	22	8.8
6	To do needful for the villagers	104	41.6
7	To provide proper guidance	1	0.4
8	1+6	3	1.2
9	2+3+4	1	0.4
10	3+4	1	0.4
11	3+6	1	0.4
12	5+6	2	0.8
13	5+7	1	0.4
14	6+7	4	1.6
	Total	250	100

Those who said about duties of panchayat representatives also, identified informal methods as source of their information about the duties. For instance, 41.2 per cent do not respond to the question, 21, 16 and 9 per cent respondents said that it is the panchayat office, villagers and the training programme through which they came to know about the duties of panchayat representative. Hence, the sources of information are both formal and informal.

So far as level of information about rights and duties of panchayat representative is concerned, majority of the respondents either do not have the knowledge (57.5%) or they feel that they are panchayat representatives but their level of knowledge about details of the panchayat is very limited.

Panchayat Election

From where the panchayat representatives came to know about the panchayat election and its specific date? It is interesting to know that here also informal sources predominated over the formal sources. For instance, 70.4 per cent came to know about panchayat election from their friends, co-villagers and husband/father. The remaining respondents had information from the formal sources like panchayat representatives, school teachers and village level government officials.

Training Programme

It is difficult to change socio-political environment suiting to the ongoing decentralization process through the Panchayti-Raj institution overnight, but in relative term, the panchayat representatives working at the village level, who are comparatively less resourceful in comparison to their J.P. and Z.P. level counterparts, may be relatively empowered and their capacity to comprehend the reality and its management may definitely be increased particularly through constant training programme. Many studies support this remark. Perhaps it is because of this reason that training programmes are organized for panchayat representatives at different levels on regular basis by both formal and informal bodies.

But in our case it is amazing that 52 per cent respondents did not attend training programme. Fourty-seven per cent attended it for maximum upto 10 days and only 2 attended it for more than 10 days. Further, 112 attended a single training programme, 7 attended 2 and the remaining 3 attended 3 training programme. Hence, maximum number of respondents either did not attend training programme at all or those who attended it, they could attend a single day training programme.

Majority from those who attended the training programme, i.e. 70 out of 122, said that such programme should continue in future and on sometime interval they should again be allowed to attend the programme.

Further, 28 said that by attending training programme their level of awareness have significantly increased. 85 respondents specifically said that today they know in detail about PR only because of the training programme. Only 9 respondents did not gain anything from the training programme.

How to ensure effectiveness of the training programme? Majority of the respondents (85%) opined that if the programme is constantly organized at the village/JP level, if informal techniques are employed and if transportation facility is provided to ensure larger participation, the outcome of the programme may be more effective and meaningful.

On the basis of above analysis it is clear that whether it is election date, awareness about rights and duties of panchayat representatives or problems of the villagers, the level of information is low and in most of the cases it is the informal sources from which they know about panchayat institution. In response to a question that how the level of awareness of panchayat representatives may be increased, respondents suggested various efforts. For instance, 21.6 per cent said that panchayat itself should provide information to its representatives. This can be done by organizing awareness camp/training programme on continuous basis. They also said that people and the representative will take interest in panchayat provided voice of the poor is properly heard, *gram sabha* meeting is timely organized and frequent interaction with change agents are encouraged. In short, respondents suggested that both formal and informal techniques should be initiated to enhance the level of awareness of panchayat representatives about different aspects of Panchayati Raj institutions.

IV

ACHIEVEMENT AND EXPECTATION

Achievement may be perceived both subjectively and objectively. It depends on the background of the perceiver. Also, there are both material and non-physical/material aspect of achievement. In the case of Panchayati Raj most often while describing achievement the representatives and others only narrate the material/physical work like construction work done by them. They seldom mention efforts leading to socio-cultural development. This is because it is easy to show material development to the villagers. Hence, objective of this section is to examine the type and level of development in both material and non-material life done by the panchayat representatives. In order to bring objectivity in the views expressed by the Panchayat representatives attempt was made to compare it with the views expressed by "others" as well as information available in the secondary sources. Similarly expectation is also subjective and dynamic. It varies from person to person in terms of its types and levels. To what extent the level of expectation is individualistic or collective and related to material or non-material development, are some of the broad issues, which have been examined in this section.

Panchayat Election

Under the new Panchayati-Raj system first election was held in 1994. Since, the area under study is numerically dominated by the tribals, therefore, it is not that for the first time the tribals joined panchayat institution in the election of 1999, rather, in 1994 election also significant number of respondents (24.8%) contested election. However, about 75 per cent of respondents joined PRI either as a member or as a president in the election of 1999. Hence, it is clear that in spite of reservation facility since 1994 election, the number of panchayat representatives from tribal community did not remain constant in the election of 1999 rather its number increased in a significant manner.

Those of the respondents who did not contest 1994 election gave number of reasons for it. For instance, 7 were of underage, 56 did not contest because the seat was not reserved for ST, 64 had no information about election, 20 did not contest election because their close relatives had contested election, 31 did not contest because at that time they had no interest in village level politics and the remaining 10 did not contest because they had no spare time for others. Hence, majority of the respondents did not contest the 1994 Panchayat election mainly due to personal reasons.

Those who contested 1994 election (62), 57 won the election. They won the election by different votes, but majority of them (45) were elected unopposed, 3 were elected by the margin of about 10 votes and the remaining 8 were elected because they received between 10-50 more votes than their counterparts. Also, those who were defeated (5) they received about 10-50 less vote than their opponent. They said that they were defeated because their opponent was from the same tribe and also from the same locality. But 2 of them said that they were defeated because their opponent used unethical practice to win the election. On this basis, it is clear that in most of the cases candidates were elected unopposed in 1994 election. This was perhaps, because majority of the candidates did not show interest in panchayat election, mainly because of their unawareness/lack of interest in the Panchayati-Raj institution.

In response to a question that by what margin the respondents were elected in the election of 1999 majority (171) were elected unopposed. Also, in case of others the margin was between 10 to 50 votes. This shows that the area under study is still homogeneous, cooperative and competition for panchayat position and political power is yet to reach there. The respondents also expressed views about the defeat of their nearest rival in the election. For example, while 171 respondents were elected unopposed and 26 did not pass their comments, the remaining respondents said that it was poor performance of the previous panchayat representatives in the past, his/her unfriendly behaviour and friendship between the elected candidates that the voters helped the new candidate to win 1999 election. This is clear from Table 4.10.

Eliticisation of Panchayat Representative

Generally it is said that as the elective bodies becomes old and mature and as people's awareness about its powers and functions becomes visible and strong gradually relatively less resourceful panchayat representatives are replaced by relatively more resourceful people. But, in this study this assumption becomes untrue. While, 76 per cent felt that in terms of background and the social status there is no difference between the representative of 1994 and 1999, but 21.6 per cent even observe that relatively more poor people were elected in 1999 election in comparison to previous election of 1994. Hence, in the area under study panchayat institution is headed by common man including relatively poor people. And, it seems that the process of replacement of non-elite by the elite in PR institution at the village level is not at all visible.

Table 4.10 : Causes of defeat of opponent and self victory as perceived by respondents

S. No.	Response	Frequency	%
1	No reply/No Response	26	10.4
2	Poor performance in past	14	5.6
3	Voters helped enthusiastically	12	4.8
4	Husband cooperation	1	0.4
5	Proper rapport with voters	6	2.4
6	Unfriendly behaviour of opponent	17	6.8
7	Elected unopposed	171	68.4
8	Opponent was illiterate	1	0.4
9	5+6	1	0.4
10	2+5	1	0.4
	Total	250	100

Reasons to Contest Election

Respondents decided to contest the panchayat election due to more than one reason, but in many of the cases (112) election was contested because candidates were requested by villagers again and again to contest. Sixty-six respondents decided to contest because of the availability of reservation facility otherwise they would not have contested. Some respondents (18) contested because of their interest in politics and similar number of them are panchayat representatives since long, therefore, they decidea to retain it. Contrary to this, only 14 respondents contested election to promote development process in the village. This is clear from Table 4.11.

Table 4.11 : Reasons behind contest in election

S. No.	Response	Frequency	%
1	No response/No reply	17	6.8
2	Reservation facility	66	26.4
3	Interest in Politics	18	7.2
4	Request by people	112	44.8
5	Panchayat representative since long	18	7.2
6	To promote development	14	5.6
7	For bright future	4	1.6
8	5+7	1	0.4
	Total	250	100

While contesting the election, respondents received cooperation from different corners. For example, 63 and 155 respondents said that family members motivated them to contest the election and in the course of election campaign also they helped them in many ways to win the election. So far as role of villagers is concerned for 152, they created atmosphere to elect them unopposed and for 82 they cooperated by casting their votes in their favour. So far as role of local level government official is concerned, their role is also visible in the total election process. 104 said that like others they also motivated them to contest. But, in case of the remaining respondents the role of government official was not visible.

Efforts to Win Election

After submitting nomination papers and declaring themselves as the candidate, respondents adopted different techniques to win the election. For instance, some people said that due to better performance in the past, they were liked and helped by the voters. In case of 22 respondents serious campaign was made by them. Similarly 78 respondents approached the voters individually. Only 4 respondents submitted that they used money power to win the election. This is clear from Table 4.12.

116 respondents feel that by becoming panchayat representatives they have done right thing. 98 are indifferent on this issue and the remaining 36 replied in the negative. Those who replied in the affirmative said that since they are panchayat representatives, they will solve people's problem successfully and

complete the on-going development work successfully. The remaining 36 respondents who replied in the negative said that they dislike this position because, even after doing work they are criticized and their social status have deteriorated. Nine respondents are unable to do their own work, mainly because of paucity of time or because of status consciousness. Nineteen respondents said that they are unable to work smoothly due to lack of cooperation from the co-workers.

Table 4.12 : Efforts to win election

S. No.	Response	Frequency	%
1	Helped people	1	0.4
2	People liked since long	4	1.6
3	Due to past performance	8	3.2
4	Nothing (Unopposed)	117	46.8
5	Helped in Panchayat work in t- past	4	1.6
6	Worked done by father/husband	3	1.2
7	Serious campaign	22	8.8
8	Proper social work	1	0.4
9	Approached voters individually	78	31.2
10	Spent money	4	1.6
11	8+10	8	3.2
	Total	250	100

People's Expectations

Except 26.8 per cent respondents villagers have variety of expectation from them. Most of these expectations are pertaining to construction work. Some want drainage problem, water problem to be solved by them and some (76) want village development by them. This is clear from Table 4.13.

Are the respondents performing as per the demand of the villagers? In response to this, 63 replied in the affirmative, 81 in the negative and the remaining 106 did not respond to this question. Those who replied in the affirmative said that since they have constructed school building, village road, arranged hand-pump, provided drainage facility, helped the villagers to get loan sanctioned for house construction, helped them to get their name included in BPL list and worked for village development, therefore, they have done work as per people's demand.

Table 4.13 : People's expectation from the Panchayat Representatives

S. No.	Response	Frequency	%
1	No Knowledge/No Reply	28	11.2
2	Construction of school building	1	0.4
3	Solution of water problem	10	4
4	Inclusion of name in BPL list	1	0.4
5	Road construction	5	2
6	Arrangement of hospital	0	0
7	No expectation	67	26.8
8	Village development	76	30.4
9	Everybody want work	51	20.4
10	Solution of drainage problem	0	0
11	2+3	2	0.8
12	2+3+5	1	0.4
13	2+5+10	1	0.4
14	3+10	1	0.4
15	3+5	4	1.6
16	4+5	1	0.4
17	5+6	1	0.4
	Total	250	100

Those not working as per the villagers' demand reasoned that partly because of shortage of fund (13), non-cooperation from sarpanch (12) and no help from local MLA (1). They (mostly panches) are incapable to fulfil villagers' demand.

Next Election

Whether the panchayat representatives are performing as per the demand or not it is different matter, but 42 per cent of them (105) say that they will surely contest the next panchayat election. 67 did not pass comment and the remaining 78 said that they will not contest the next election. Those who will contest the next election, 14 of them did not mention the reason but about 24 per cent said that they will contest it for people's welfare and development. Thirty respondents said that currently they are panch and nobody listen to panch, therefore, they will contest for sarpanch post for the cause of villagers. Those who replied in the negative said that due to criticism of people (11), personal loss (1), status deterioration (14), loss of wages work (8), lack of desire (9), and lack of cooperation from family members (9), they will not contest the next panchayat election.

As stated earlier, 105 will contest the next panchayat election but many of them will contest for higher level position for instance, Panch will contest for Sarpanch post and significant number of Panches will take decision on this issue after seeing that which post is reserved for them and which not. Only few respondents (7) think to contest for JP/ZP level membership. This is clear from the following Table 4.14.

Table 4.14 : Contest for which post

S. No.	Response	Frequency	%
1	No response	1	0.4
2	Not applicable	145	58
3	Undecided	5	2
4	Sarpanch	30	12
5	As per reservation facility	38	15.2
6	Panch	23	9.2
7	J.P. Member	6	2.4
8	Z.P. Member	1	0.4
9	4+7	1	0.4
	Total	250	100

Those who will contest the next election feel that people will cast vote in their favour, because of variety of reasons. 20 said that they will vote to complete the ongoing work, 24 feel that since their performance is as per the desire of people, therefore, people will prefer them. 21 and 16 feel that they will be able to seek vote due to friendly relation as well as better performance in the past. The remaining respondents were either indifferent on this issue or they said that because of more than one reason voters will prefer their candidature in the next election.

Achievement

About 39.2 per cent respondents did not feel that they have done some concrete work as a panchayat representative. Majority of the representatives, however, have done work in panchayat.

Maximum number of them (45) said that village road was constructed by them. Also, some of the respondents provided handump, tank and school building facility to the villagers. Some respondents opined that they constructed more than one structure of different type. For instance, 11 respondents constructed village road and drainage system. Similar number of them constructed road and provided handpump facility. In other words, majority of the respondents constructed road along with some other activities like village bridge, panchayat building, water tank, *choupal* etc. However, work for the development of people from health, education and women's empowerment point of view was done not even by couple of respondents. This shows that for the representatives, development refers to merely construction work and did not include social, economic and cultural aspects of life under the umbrella of development. It is possible that they might have done some work in this area, but they do not consider such work under the purview of development.

In response to a question that how the work was completed and from where fund was made available, 98 respondents did not respond to the question. Majority of them were panches who are practically seldom associated with development activities. From the remaining respondents 60 said that fund was made available from JRY fund for this purpose. Also, 46 said that it was the panchayat institution which provided financial support from different sources. So far as completion of work by people's voluntary cooperation is concerned, hardly 12 representatives could receive it. The role of NGO is absent in the area under study and whatever development has taken place neither it is from the local level available resource nor from the local influential. Rather, it is only from the government departments. This is clear from Table 4.15.

Respondents received disproportionate amount of cooperation in completion of the work done by them during last couple of years. For example, 184, 211, 8, 185, 52 and 207 respondents received maximum amount of cooperation from the co-representatives, villagers, NGO, caste panchayat, government officials and family members respectively. On this basis it seems that formal sources like co-representatives and government officials were not as

Table 4.15 : How works were completed?

S. No.	Response	Frequency	%
1	No response/Not applicable	98	39.2
2	JRY fund	60	24
3	Help from J.P. Member	11	4.4
4	Help from Political Parties	2	0.8
5	Help from Panchayat	46	18.4
6	People's cooperation	11	4.4
7	MLA/MP fund	2	0.8
8	Government. aid	12	4.8
9	NGO's help	1	0.4
10	3+5	1	0.4
11	5+6	3	1.2
12	5+8	1	0.4
13	6+8	2	0.8
	Total	250	100

co-operative as the informal sources like villagers, caste panchayat and family members. In contrary to this, role of NGO is insignificant in the life of panchayat representatives. It is needless to mention that we chould identify the existence of only two NGOs in the study area. This suggests that in order to strengthen interface between panchayat and its representatives, from performance point of view, there is need to strengthen the role of formal organization and retain the contribution of informal sources. This is clear from Table 4.16.

Table 4.16 : Level of support from different sources

Res	Other Represen-tatives		Villagers		NGO's		Caste panchayat		Govern-ment Officials		Family members	
	Fre	%	Fre	%	Fre	%	Fre	%	Fre	%	Fre	%
1	184	73.6	211	84.4	8	3.2	185	74	52	20.8	207	82.8
2	46	18.4	22	8.8	148	59.2	47	18.8	170	68	23	9.2
3	12	4.8	8	3.2	84	33.6	9	3.6	15	6	9	3.6
4	8	3.2	9	3.6	10	4	9	3.6	13	5.2	11	4.4
To-tal	250	100	250	100	250	100	250	100	250	100	250	100

Note : 1 = High, 2 = Medium, 3 = Low, 4 = NR

Incomplete Work

In certain cases due to various contradictions, development schemes are left incomplete or it is withdrawn. In this case, however, the cases of withdrawal etc. is very less. For instance, only 3 respondents said that road construction was incomplete because available fund was misappropriated particularly by Sarpanch and his men. In one case, handpump facility was withdrawn because of infighting among the expected beneficiaries.

Experience

Representatives experienced both positive and negative taste in panchayat work. While significant number of them (79) particularly Panch did not have any specific experience, 41 said that they have friendly relations with villagers and co-workers and they are respected by them. 38 said that their level of knowledge about village problem have drastically increased during the couple of years. In contrary to this, 51 respondents said that nobody listen to them, they have personal loss and they are also criticized by the villagers. Most of the respondents having bad taste in panchayat are panch. The remaining respondents shared more than one positive or negative experience in Panchayati-Raj.

Respondents also provided comparative picture in comparison to another panchayat representative, in terms of their performance. While, 72 did not respond to this question, 110 said that their performance level is like others. 33 and 35 respondents rated themselves either above or below to the co-representatives respectively. They gave different logics to support their stand point. For example, 58 said that in terms of grant, people's cooperation and personal quality, they are at par with other representatives, therefore, at the performance level also, there is similarity. Some respondents said that their performance is better because they have more commitment and they received more grants incomparison to others. Those who rank themselves below accused sarpanch for their manipulation and received grant very late, therefore, they did not do visible work.

Expectation

Panchayat representatives have different level and type of expectation from different corners. For example, they want villagers cooperation and participation to undertake and complete development work in time. None of them observe that the villagers should give taxes to the panchayat, in order to make panchayat economically self-reliant. But the nature of desired cooperation from government official is completely economic in nature. 171 respondents said that they should arrange maximum grant for the panchayat and 43 said that such grant should be quickly released to the panchayat. Respondents (216) need cooperation from the co-representatives of different caste and class either belonging to their own panchayat or outside it. From NGO they need campaign which can ensure awareness and capacity building of the villagers.

Indicators of Development

Development is a value loaded concept. Therefore, each of the respondents have their own definition of development. Also, there are more than one indicators of development. It is interesting to note that for 115 respondents if villagers are properly informed about the development schemes by the panchayat, it can serve basis for their development. Many respondents, however, confused development with construction. They said that so long as number of constructions are not made in panchayat villages such villages cannot be termed as developed. Further, proper water facility, employment opportunity at the local level, construction and availability of school facility is also perceived as indicators of development. Therefore, respondents are thinking to do some concrete construction work in the remaining period of their tenure. For instance, many of them plan to provide school, road, drinking water, community hall, village bridge, panchayat building, health centre, drainage and well/handpump facility to the people. Further, 42 respondents had not planned as yet that what they will do in future, significant number of respondents think that they will try their best to ensure benefits of development to the people. Here also, respondents confused development with construction because large number of them said that construction of road is a pre-condition for village development. None of the respondents have any plan for the development of women, children, aged, handicapped and chronically poor inhabitants of their panchayat.

How they will actualize their plan for development? In response to this question 23.2 per cent respondents did not pass comments and the remaining have either disclosed one or more than one strategy. For instance, 15 said that they have already submitted proposal at the higher level, 12 said that they will try to seek villagers cooperation in this regard 28 will have yet to decide, the remaining 47 said that with the help of government fund they will deal with the issues. 77 respondents said that they will actualize their dream with the cooperation of co-representative in the panchayat.

Efforts/Precautions for Development

Sixty-two respondents said that some extra budget should be allotted to panchayat by the government so that along with new work, the incomplete work may also be completed within time. 56 said that number of development works should be increased by the government two to three times. 42 said that there must be training programme for the development agents in order to enhance their level of awareness and to develop feeling of cooperation. 52 respondents did not pass comments. Some respondents said that there should be devolution of power of sarpanch to the level of panch to ensure their effective participation. To them today panchs are the passive participants in the PR system. Some said that if the feeling of dedication, road facility etc. is made, the village will retain or increase the pace of development. There is also need to take some precaution in order to ensure panchayat induced development process. For instance, 74 respondents said that corruption should be checked and change agents should be encouraged to work honestly. Similarly, the rate of development can be increased provided feeling of cooperation is strengthened among different stakeholders.

Comparison between Tribal and Non-tribal Representatives

Can the tribal representatives do more justice to the tribal population in comparison to the non-tribal representative? 126 respondents do not see any difference between tribal and non-tribal representatives. They argued that not only today but even before the introduction of 73rd Constitutional amendment large number of tribals were in the PRI in Betul. Like today in the past also their background was similar to that of the villagers. But in spite of that development remained dream in the life of most of the tribals. But large number of respondents are of the opinion that due to lack of sensitivity on the part of non-tribal representatives to the problems of tribal, the development of the tribal under their leadership is not possible. Only the tribal representatives can do justice to the tribal population. This is clear from Table 4.17.

Table 4.17 : Comparison between tribal and non-tribal representatives

S.No.	Response	Frequency	%
1	No response	7	2.8
2	No difference	126	50.4
3	No work at all	18	7.2
4	Lack of sensitivity	11	4.4
5	Stagnation of development process	57	22.8
6	No respect	6	2.4
7	No benefit from the scheme	23	9.2
8	5+7	1	0.4
9	6+7	1	0.4
	Total	250	100

But if we examine the above two tables dealing with achievement and performance by tribal representatives, the validity of opinions expressed through Table 4.9 becomes doubtful. This is because like others, tribal representatives also confuse construction with development and they do not address the basic questions related to social and economic life of common tribal population. The question of dropout and non-enrollment, high mortality rate, economic insecurity, mal-nutrition, movement from dependent livelihood to independent livelihood, cultural disintegration etc. which are some of the specific problems of the tribals are seldom addressed by village level tribal leadership. In course of our study we could not see even a single panchayat which is primarily dealing with the basic social and cultural problems of poor tribals.

Major Difficulties in Performance

From the point of view of existing parameters of development the panchayats under study are underdeveloped, therefore, lot of efforts is needed to achieve development. But about 50 per cent respondents do not see difficulty in their work and 18.8 per cent see lack of grant as the main source of difficulty. 19.6 per cent accuse poor condition of basic facility of village, which stagnate their efforts for development. For 8 representatives, sarpanch is the main source of the difficulty. Hence, panchayat representatives have to experience difficulties from various sources.

How to overcome these difficulties? 126 did not respond to this question. 43 advised that the problems may be minimized provided grants are increased and released at the earliest. 47 respondents feel that currently the type of cooperation from the government official is not upto the mark. It should be increased and for this training programme for them should also be organized every now and then. Some of the respondents said that the problem may be minimized provided sarpanch is not allowed to do as per his own liking and disliking. Respondents also said that people in large number do not attend the *gram sabha* meeting. Hence, there should be such meetings in each village and villagers should be motivated to attend meeting without any fail. They also said that in comparison to past, today less number of villagers attend *gram sabha* meeting. They want gain, but due to shortage of fund and delay in its release people gradually loose faith in *gram sabha*, hence, they are not interested to attend the *gram sabha* meeting. Therefore, respondents said that concrete work needs to be done by both government and the panchayat to ensure larger participation. Also, *gram sabha* meeting should be organized not so frequently, because it affects the poor and wage earner negatively. The opinions of respondents are clear from Table 4.18.

Table 4.18 : Suggestions to solve village level problem

S. No	Response	Freq.	%
1	No response/Not applicable	126	50.4
2	Sarpanch should be punished	5	2
3	People should be motivated to attend Gram Sabha meeting	4	1.6
4	Grants should be released in time	43	17.2
5	Gram Sabha meeting should not be so frequent	2	0.8
6	Government officials should be sensitive	47	18.8
7	1+4	12	4.8
8	2+6	10	4
9	3+6	1	0.4
	Total	250	100

More specifically, about 35 per cent respondents accept that people are not interested to attend *gram sabha* meeting because (a) there is no proper seating arrangement at the meeting place, (b) people do not understand importance of the meeting, therefore, they do not attend it, (c) about 11 respondents feel that people have to loose time and wage, if they attend the meeting, (d) due to fear of criticism secretary also, do not attend the meeting, and (e) some people deliberately do not attend the meeting because to them it is not beneficial. Due to lack of any gain from the *gram sabha* meeting over the time they have lost faith and interest in it.

Economic Gain

Panchayat work has economically affected the panchayat representatives in insignificant manner. About 90 per cent respondents do not see negative or positive impact of their involvement in panchayat work, on their economic condition. On the other side, only 2 respondents said that their economic condition is now better and 20 feel that it has deteriorated due to job loss.

Gram Kosh

58.8 per cent respondents do not know the concept of *gram kosh*. 5 said that they know about it partially because sarpanch and secretary do not inform them about it. 35.6 per cent respondents, however, feel that the condition of *gram kosh* is upto the mark. Also, 6 said that flow of income in *gram kosh* is regular.

Dispute Management

In spite of statutory institutions at the village and block level, people at large still manage dispute of minor nature at the village level. It is the elders, local influential, family friends and neighbour, who initiate negotiations. The role of mutual understanding between the parties is significant in this context. The gram panchayat has still to show its visibility in this matter.

Women's Participation

It is true that there is 33 per cent reservation for women in the Panchayati-Raj and they are available at all the three levels of panchayat, but so far as the extent of their participation in day-to-day decision making process is concerned, it is not upto the mark. About 74 per cent respondents, who are both men and women, opined this view. Only 4 respondents feel that level of their participation is high. 53 respondents think that the level is neither high nor low.

Respondents gave number of suggestions to increase their level of participation. For instance, 53 feel that only constant awareness campaign can ensure their participation. For 27, by solving their day-to-day problem the participation level may be increased. Further, by making them literate, by making them critical citizen and by providing various inputs, level of their participation in panchayat activities may be increased.

On the basis of above discussion it may be concluded that today due to reservation facility large number of tribals have joined the PRI in different capacity. Their level of understanding of PRI have increased over the time. The role of training programme is significant in this context. Many of them have done significant work as a PRI representatives. Many are interested to contest the next Panchayat election. But their concept of development is narrow because they do not distinguish construction and development. And if construction is development then for its actualization they have totally to depend on the government fund. Since the fund is scarce, the sanctioned fund is not released in time, therefore the impact of development process is also not visible. All of them are failed to generate resources at the local level. Their low level of development is contributed by their poor socio-economic background, lack of awareness and lack of possible cooperation from the *gram sabha* members, fellow representatives and the bureaucracy. This calls for, besides other •input, training programme, particularly through informal way for all the representatives, local level officials, Panchayat Secretary and others on constant basis.

V

OTHERS PERCEPTIONS

In order to maintain objectivity and transparency in the study, it is essential that opinions of tribal panchayat representatives regarding the functioning and achievement of panchayat under their leadership must be verified from different sources. In this context it is essential that views of some of the members of *gram sabha* and local level government officials associated with panchayat activities should be collected. If the views of panchayat representatives are broadly similar to the views of the above mentioned respondents, it can be inferred that the responses provided by the representatives are closer to the reality. For this purpose we interviewed cross-section of population. Their views are analyzed and presented in the following manner.

Perception of Gram Sabha Members

An attempt was made to analyse the views of tribal and non-tribal members of *Gram Sabha*. Views of 9 tribal and 11 non-tribal *Gram Sabha* members were finally comprehended. Most of the interviewed villagers have land and they are engaged in agricultural activities. Most of the time they live in the villages. They are both illiterate and educated and belong to the age group of 25-59 years.

About 80 per cent respondents feel that in comparison to the functioning of previous gram panchayat, the functioning of current gram panchayat is bad. It is bad because functioning of sarpanch is confined to his own *mohallah*, he is failed to provide pension and homestead land to the people. The sarpanch have completely neglected other villages and *mohallah*, whatever they have done in the last few years it is only confined to the small locality. Fagulal (ST) said that his sarpanch is from other village. He has done work only in his own village. He is useless fellow. Whatever direction he receives from Secretary, he has to do. So long as he retains the post of Sarpanch development work is impossible. Another respondent of the similar background also said that "Secretary is everything. Sarpanch is only the signature master." Most of the community members interviewed by us replied in the same manner. A tribal villager from Danora Panchayat accused that "performance of previous Sarpanch was much better in comparison to the present one. Since the village is tribal dominated therefore the seat was reserved. He was asked to contest the election by his non-tribal master (*Malik*). He works as per the direction of his *malik* and the secretary. He can do nothing at his own."

But about 20 per cent respondents feel that Panchayat has done significant work by constructing village road and solving water problem. Hence, its functioning is not poor and inferior in comparison to the functioning of previous leadership. If we look into the overall functioning of the current gram panchayat, almost all the respondents, however, observe that the concerned panchayat has done more than one work. For instance, 4 respondents said that their panchayats have constructed village road and deepening work of village pond. 8 respondents shared this view and said that it has also constructed additional rooms in the existing school. About equal number of them said that besides the above, it has provided house to a small number of homeless people, constructed water line, dam and provided community drinking water facility. In short, all the community members feel that panchayats have done mainly the construction works. Works related to health, education, poverty eradication, awareness programme etc. have not been done by these panchayats. Therefore, all the respondents feel that such developmental activities are not sufficient from the point of view of sustainable and total development of the village. They reasoned that besides the above work if a veterinary hospital, water tank, high school, village road, drainage facility is not constructed, panchayat do not maintain honesty in its functioning and anti-encroachment drive is not launched, panchayat cannot be rated as successful.

So far as impact of tribal leadership on village harmony and inter-caste relationship is concerned, respondents expressed mixed views. While 40 per cent (8) said that there is no impact, the other 40 per cent feel that sarpanch is only show piece. He has no independent stand. The remaining 20 per cent said that under the current leadership there is overall deterioration in the village condition.

Gram Sabha Meeting

Since the functioning of Panchayat is not very strong and beneficial to the people, therefore, about 60 per cent respondents do not attend *Gram Sabha* meeting. Villager Barigram (SC) seldom attend *Gram Sabha* meeting. This is because everybody discusses irrelevant matter. Nobody listen to anybody. Only *Samiti* members do some work. First, the Panch should attend the meeting then only others will attend. There are other causative factors such as lack of information, only formal meeting, lack of solution of problems etc., which are of vital importance. All these factors collectively contribute to absenteeism. 8 respondents attend the meeting because they have their say in the meeting and they receive intimation in time. Commenting on the functioning of *Gram Sabha* Budhi Bai (SC) said, "I never attended the *Gram Sabha* meeting. I am failed to know when and where the meeting is organised. Sarpanch either conduct secret meeting at his place or ask only few to put signature without meeting."

However, most of them gave suggestions for effective functioning of *Gram Sabha*. They said that if sarpanch is educated, panches are encouraged to attend the meeting, secretary is directed to provide correct information to the villagers, no personal/political discussion in meeting is held and if *gram panchayat* and sarpanch honestly work, surely people at large will realize its importance, participate in the meeting and can contribute to its functioning in the meaningful manner.

Tribal Leaders

Respondents at large feel that tribal society is not at all significantly different in terms of its development under the new leadership of its own community members. This is because not only this leadership is illiterate, dependent and poor, but also they lack consciousness and many of them are elected unopposed. They are elected unopposed not because there is consensus among the villagers on their candidature but because people are unconscious and indifferent. Villagers at large do not understand the meaning and importance of Panchayati-Raj. They also said that in 80 per cent cases it is the secretary who matters in the panchayat. In most of the cases level of education and awareness of secretary is higher than that of the elected representatives. In the remaining cases decision is taken by the *gram sabha*. All our 20 respondents feel that panchayat representatives cannot take independent decisions. It is needless to mention that people expressed mixed views about the role of panchayat secretary. Only few said that he is doing well but most of our respondents said that he performs as per his desire. In several cases, he himself do the work of sarpanch. G.P. Sarley of Danora Panchayat said, "Secretary is everything. Sarpanch is nothing. Sarpanch is illiterate. He is easily manipulated by the educated secretary. Secretary has encroached community land. He managed pension for his father who is a railway employee and already getting pension, from the social security scheme. No body is raising voice. Sarpanch is silent on those issues."

People have some expectation from the panchayat. About 50 per cent observed that panchayat should function in an honest manner and it should also motivate others to perform honestly. However, it was suggested that by motivation only work can be taken from all the concerned. It was also suggested that besides honesty on the part of all the Panachayat functionaries it is essential that through regular training, the awareness level of both panch and sarpanch should be increased. Each panch or sarpanch must have clear idea about the problem of village.

Table: 4.19 : Major problems in Panchayat villages (multiple response)

Response	Frc.	%
Lack of drinking water, electricity and high school	2	10
Lack of drinking water, electricity, incidence of encroachment and connecting road	3	15
Lack of drinking water, electricity and health centre	4	20
Lack of drinking water and problem of encroachment	6	30
Lack of electricity, health centre and deforestation	5	25
Total	20	100

Problems in Villages

In course of study regarding some of the major problems in the villages it was observed that drinking water, electricity, encroachment of the government land, lack of health facility, lack of school and problem of deforestation etc., prominently figured in the list provided by the community members. This is clear from Table 4.19.

Reservation Facility and Tribal Leadership

None of our 20 respondents perceive reservation as a sufficient condition for the empowerment of tribal masses in general and tribal leadership in particular. This is because reservation can only provide position. Since most of the Panchayat representatives are poor and illiterate, therefore, panchayat and its functioning is only taken by the tribal leaders in a routinised manner. There is limited space for being assertive. It is a general comment by the community members that tribal leadership in PRI lack capacity to take independent decision.

Panchayat and NGO

The area under study lack NGO. There is hardly two NGOs in the entire Janpad area, namely *World Vision* and RICHA, 60 per cent respondents do not see visibility of these two NGOs in terms of its functioning. The remaining 40 per cent said that it has repaired handpump, constructed toilet in school and also constructed filter plant for drainage. However, they do not differentiate between these NGOs and the contractor in terms of taking villagers into confidence while performing construction work. In other words these NGOs seldom encourage villagers to participate in the development process.

Panchayat and Women

One of the duties of PRI is to empower women and protect the rights of children. But in this case as per the perception of 60 per cent respondents till date no work has been done so far. In some of the villages only *anganwadi* work was introduced by the panchayat and till date only small number of women have received training for income generation.

Perceptions of Government Officials

Ten government officials working at the Panchayat and the Block level and directly dealing with panchayat activities were interviewed to know their perception about the functioning of panchayat. Half of them replied in the negative and half in the positive. Those who replied in the positive said that since the current representatives have done more work in comparison to the previous leadership in terms of road construction, handpump, housing and drinking water facility, since they are helpful to all and they function in an objective manner, therefore, their work can be rated positively. But this does not mean that if the reservation facility is lifted they will win the election. About 80 per cent respondents see this possibility out of question. This is more so because most of them are illiterate, they are poor with having low socio-economic status and therefore, they cannot compete with others. Hence, reservation is must for ensuring them elected in the PRI. A Panchayat Secretary said, "The general caste people are influential. Without reservation facility, they will never allow the tribals to become Sarpanch. The present Sarpanch of Bharush Panchayat is illiterate. He works as per the dictates of others. He cannot take decision. But the educated Sarpanch apply their own brain." Similar observation was made by the B.D. Soni, a Panchayat Inspector. But a tribal village assistant said, "Besides illiteracy it is poverty and their involvement in wage work, as a result neither they may win the election without reservation nor they may take independent decision in Panchayat activities.

Since tribal leadership is neither very active nor innovative and different in comparison to non-tribal leadership, therefore, their impact on tribal development is also not significantly different. Most of the works done by the tribal leaders are works related to construction. Like other representatives they also do not have clear idea of and faith in social development. However, a new trend under their leadership is that today tribal women do not hesitate to narrate their problems before tribal leaders in the meeting of *gram sabha*. They are very comfortable in narrating their problems in their dialect. One of the non-ST Panchayat Secretaries said, "Of course, there is no fundamental improvement in the life of the tribals under the tribal leadership but since Sarpanch is from their own community, therefore, they freely narrate their problems which was otherwise not possible." Jitendra Soni, Secretary, said that now in contrary to past women do not hesitate to come out and narrate before the Panchayat. Referring to impact on women one of the Panchayat Inspectors said, "Women are now more aware. In the past the government had to put pressure on them to attend family planning devices but today they themselves discuss these and other development issues." It was also reported that besides similarity between tribal and non-tribal leadership in terms of addressing tribal problem, tribal leaders are more sensitive to it and if proper input is provided to them through training and resources, definitely their contribution for the mitigation of tribal problem will become obvious. Respondents suggested that role of tribal leaders may be effective provided reservation facility already available in the reserved panchayat is made relatively durable, allotted fund is released in time, bureaucracy is discouraged to interfere, and training is made regular feature. Importance of training is vital because all the respondents observed that those who have gone through training programme they have more knowledge about panchayat, their level of information about schemes have increased and there is overall improvement in their understanding and functioning.

Role of NGO

Since the officials interviewed have wider area of operation, therefore, they have perceived functioning of panchayat in a broader context. To 8 of them, most of the NGOs are engaged in number of activities such as construction of school building, platform of handpump, seating arrangement in school, construction of boundary wall of schools and so on. Further, they have provided toilet facility, formed Self-Help Group and launched watershed and cleanliness drive. Hence, as per their perception the role of NGO is very obvious in rural development. But to them also NGO do little for social development of the poor and the ignorant tribals.

Tribal Problem

All the respondents said that there are some common and some specific problems encountered by most of the tribals in the district of Betul in general and in Betul Development Block in particular. Some of these problems are lack of village road, water problem, unemployment, education, electricity, village bridge, health centre, environmental pollution, housing and so on. This is clear from Table 4.20.

Table 4.20 : Basic problems of tribal villages? (Multiple response)

Response	Fre.	%
Inspiration to move up	1	10
Road, water and housing	1	10
Road, water, education and high inspiration	1	10
Road, water, health facility and electricity	1	10
Road and village bridge	1	10
Road and water	1	10
Road, water and electricity	1	10
Water, education and health	1	10
Education, health, environmental pollution, water and road	1	10
Electricity, water and road	1	10
Total	10	100

In response to the question that who (tribal or non-tribal leaders) can contribute more to tribal development, it was reported by 80 per cent respondents that both–tribal and non-tribal-respondents can equally do the needful in this direction. Tribal leaders alone cannot address the problem because the nature of the problem is very complex and it requires attack from different corners. It was stated that if honesty is maintained in the work, elected representatives are trusted, they are provided training regularly and fund is regularly increased then only tribal problems can be addressed in a meaningful manner.

Problem Before Tribal Leadership

The emerging tribal leadership have many problems to face. Few important among these are both from within and outside. For example, non-cooperation from officials and other representatives and pressure from non-tribal population are outside constraints. Panchayat Secretary of Vadras G.P. said that high officials do not extend cooperation to the tribal leaders honestly. Even the non-tribal Panch do not extend cooperation. Dilip Hazare, another Panchayat Secretary said that due to (a) fearness and lack of self-confidence, (b) lack of experience, and (c) lack of cooperation from officials and the non-tribal fellow representatives, the tribal sarpanch is failed to do meaningful in Panchayat. Similar observation was made by another secretary. To him "The representatives of the general category working at the J.P. and Z.P. level discourage the genuine proposal of the tribal leaders. Since the tribal leaders are illiterate, therefore, they are failed to present their case properly. They have to face interference from different corners. This discourage them to do sincerely." Illiteracy, economic crisis, feeling of insecured future and lack of interest in work due to unemployment etc., inhibit them to do meaningful work in the PRI. Since, problems are from different corners, therefore, they expect solution of these problems from different corners. It was observed that if proper help is extended by the officials, non-tribal leaders extend help, regular training is provided to them and if people in *gram sabha* help at all the levels, corruption is constantly attacked then only problems of tribal representatives can be reduced and the road for their progress and effective participation can be strengthened. One of the panchayat secretaries rightly remarked that "Of course *gram sabha* meeting is monthly held but due to lack of corum, particularly due to busyness of villagers, proper and larger participation is not ensured. Even most of the Panchs do not attend the meeting." It was also suggested that by doing hard work, by imposing tax on the villagers, by seeking cooperation from the masses, by reducing the frequency of *gram sabha* meeting one in each month which kill interest to maximum upto six times in a year, the problem of tribal representatives may be reduced. It is needless to mention that today the functioning of *gram sabha* is not effective. This is because in many cases its meeting is held on paper, actual beneficiaries are neither informed nor persuaded to attend the meeting, people do not cooperate with each other in the meeting, only few panchs attend the meeting, proposals are not made in a practical manner, people are uninformed and therefore, there is lack of confidence. Therefore, *gram sabha* is not effective in anyway to help the sarpanch to take independent decisions. However, due to the meeting of *gram sabha* there is growing consciousness among the people. Those who attend the meeting they have now some idea of rights and duties of *gram sabha* and importance of *gram panchayat* in village development.

On the basis of above analysis it is clear that due to variety of historical reasons, of course, there is tribal leadership in the PRI, and many of them are as effective as others but large number of them are not capacitated to understand their rights and duties. Therefore, at the decision and action level they are dependent mainly on the panchayat secretary. As a result in many cases panchayat secretary has manipulated the situation in their own favour. Tribal representatives have done work in the panchayat, but most of these works are related to infrastructure development. These works are not sustainable in the sense that it has been done only due to government support. If the government support is not available they cannot continue construction work. And to seek government grant they have to follow all the ethical and unethical means as followed by the others. The role of training programme, reservation facility etc. is very important, but none of these are sufficient in itself. The support from *gram sabha* and NGO is also not very strong. Given the situation tribal leadership can become effective and powerful only when *gram sabha* is strengthened, common cause is addressed honestly, training programme is organised regularly, allotted fund is released in time and people's mobilization in favour of Panchayats and its activities are ensured on regular basis.

VI

CASE STUDY

Re-introduction of Panchayat institution through specific Constitutional package by the government by introducing 73rd Constitutional amendment is an effort to ensure participation of marginalised groups in the decision making process at the grassroots level. Besides the reservation facility for weaker section, provision of training programme and other interventions have been also made by the state for capacity building of the representatives. Both the tribal and the non-tribal representatives have to function in similar environment but in spite of that there is difference in their social background, level of awareness and experience in panchayat activities. How and to what extent tribal leaders have managed the situation? What are their perception, experience and plan? These are some of the issues which have been comprehended through the case-study technique. The cases selected are to a great extent similar to our 250 respondents in many ways. In other words, in spite of the fact that their actual names are produced here, but one can perceive them in common noun. The cases are mentioned below :

S.No.	Name	Position	Tribe	Land	Political affiliation	Education
1	Krishna Kumre	Sarpanch	Gond	45 Acres	BJP	Middle Class
2	Jagoti Bai	Panch	Gond	Landless	No	Literate
3	Bhuri Bai	Sarpanch	Gond	5 Acres	Congress	Literate
4	Rango Bai	J.P. President	Gond	8 Acres	Congress	Illiterate
5	Ammu Singh	Sarpanch	Gond	30 Acres	Congress	Higher Secondary

Krishna Kumre

Krishna Kumre is a 40 years old married, middle class level educated farmer. He is a Gond Sarpanch who hails from the poor family. He is the only earning hand in the family with having five dependants, although his wife helps him in agricultural activities. The family do not possess modern household and agricultural assets. The family own about 45 acres of land with having minimum level of irrigation facility. The family is not under debt.

He is an active member of BJP like his father although he seldom took part in political activities. He fought 1994 Panchayat election for Sarpanch but he was defeated by a margin of 14 votes. But he won 1999 Panchayat election by the margin of 100 votes. The sitting Sarpanch was defeated because of his poor performance in panchayat. After being elected he attended two training programmes for 6 days at the local and at the district level. But he realised that he did not learn anything out of the training programme.

Krishna is an aware Sarpanch. To him the new panchayati system was introduced for villager's development but it is failed to do so because people do not attend the *gram sabha* meeting. He has very limited knowledge of rights and duties of Sarpanch. He knows that villagers are facing problem of drinking water. There is no school building. He thinks to provide these facilities but he is helpless because everything is partially decided by the Panchayat Secretary. Sarpanch is simply asked to sign. He suggests that without enhancing the level of awareness among the masses success of panchayat cannot be ensured.

Why he became Sarpanch? He became Sarpanch because he is a simple man and villagers advised him to contest the election by looking to his simplicity. As yet he has provided drainage and road facility in the village. He is satisfied by his performance, therefore, he feels that he should recontest the next election for the same post. He is confident that because of his performance in panchayat in the current phase people will favour him in the next election.

He is an involved Sarpanch. He got some construction work done due to availability of fund from JRY. But he feels that because of panchayat work he has no spare time for himself. He is unable to get his family work done in time. He also feels that he is a better Sarpanch in comparison to his predecessor because of his overall performance. To him people at large do not attend the *gram sabha* meetings. He advised that the villagers and Panch should necessarily attend these meetings. To him so long as problems are not solved we cannot say that proper development has taken place in the village. However, the main problem in his panchayat village is lack of drinking water, school building, *anganwadi bhavan* etc. And, this can only be constructed provided fund is made available by the government. He cannot generate fund at the local level because the villagers are too poor to face this burden.

As yet whatever has been done in the panchayat, he has mainly received cooperation from co-representatives, villagers, community members and the family members. The formal organisations are yet to help him in significant manner. He feels that had there been non-tribal representative at his place he may not have done as much work as has been done by him.

He admits that women do not participate in the panchayat work. Also, even being Sarpanch he does not know the concept of *Panchayat Kosh*. However, he is successful to solve the minor dispute among the villagers at the local level informally. Finally, he advised that if *Gram Sabha* meeting is successfully organised it may solve many problems and can ensure success of panchayat.

Jagoti Bai

Jagoti Bai is a poor and middle aged literate Gond panch. She lives in a *kaccha* house, which is although electrified, but there is nothing like modern amenities. Actually she and her husband is a wage earner. The family is landless although it is free from debt. Except a bicycle there is not even a single household or agricultural asset in the family. Neither she nor any of her family members are associated with any of the political parties/social organisations. Further, before becoming panch she never attended any political activities.

Being *panch* there is radical change in her social status. Her social status is very high. People come to consult her. Even when she is on wage work people come to motivate her to attend the meeting.

She was elected as panch in 1999 election unopposed. She does not see any difference between herself and the previous panch. Also, she attended a three-day training programme. She learnt about her rights and duties. She is aware that the new PR was introduced in 1994 but she does not know its reasons. Lack of road and lack of village bridge are the main problems in her panchayat village. She admitted that for all infonnations she is dependent on the panchayat secretary. However, she suggested that by providing training facility on regular basis, the level of awareness of panchayat representatives may definitely be increased.

Villagers and family members helped her to become *panch* with the specific purpose, i.e. to get village road constructed and *patta* (land ownership document) to be distributed. But she did not do anything. She feels guilty for her non-performance. She narrates that at the cost of wage work she goes to attend the panchayat meeting but she feels frustrated to see infighting among the members. But Jagoti is hopeful people will help her to win the next election on the same post and she will do as per the requirement. She managed one school building and two handpumps in the village. This work was done from the government fund. She said that if there is mutual understanding among the *panches* and if government fund is released in time all the pending construction works like construction of village road, local bridge and *Anganwadi Bhawan* may be completed in time.

She does not see difference between the tribal panch and the non-tribal panch in terms of their work for tribal development. She does not have the information of *Gram Kosh* in the panchayat. In her village also the local problems are solved at the local level. Further in spite of being woman she is failed to enhance women's participation in panchayat activities.

Bhuri Bai

Bhuri Bai is a Sarpanch. She is fifty years old, married, literate and poor woman. Her main source of livelihood is wage work.

She lives in *kaccha* house with having no modern amenities except electricity. She is a member of Congress Party since 1990 like her husband, although as yet, she has not participated in political activities. The family owns about 5 acres of unirrigated land. She is not under debt, rather she has some savings. The family has some of the traditional households and agricultural assets.

She became Sarpanch in 1994 and before that her husband was sarpanch. In the 1999 election she defeated the nearest rival by 68 votes. The nature of relation of her opponent with the villagers was hostile, therefore, she was defeated. As yet she has not attended training programme. Since she attends the panchayat meetings and interacts with the villagers, therefore, she knows her rights and duties. She is satisfied with it. People expect from her about construction of road, handpump and houses. She advised that panchayat representatives should be provided information about panchayat at the panchayat level itself by the government officials.

She knows that it was only reservation facility which made her Sarpanch. She approached all the voters for favour and in this work her family members helped her. She is happy that by becoming Sarpanch she has done right thing because in this capacity extension work of school building was done. But she laments that she did not construct the connecting road, which passes through the thick forest. This was only due to lack of sufficient resources. However, she is hopeful that if reservation facility continues she will contest the next election and if elected she will complete the incomplete work.

As per her understanding construction refers to development. She did not do much construction work like her predecessor husband because she has received relatively less amount of grant. She is fully dependent on government grant for development work. She advised that if grant is increased and released in time, people support in the panchayat work, schemes are timely approved and the co-representatives provide help, all the pending work of panchayats like handpump facility, road construction work etc., will be done.

The village is located in very remote area. There is not even a single handpump in the entire village. People are totally dependent on *Tapti* river for drinking water. Also, there is no connecting road. Since due to lack of fund she is unable to address these problems, therefore, in spite of the fact that she spent more and more time in the panchayat activities, she is most often criticized by the villagers.

Rango Bai

Rango Bai, a Gond by tribe, is aged and illiterate woman. She is housewife and therefore do not have any personal income. There are 7 members in the family and all are engaged in the agricultural activities. The family is slightly above the poverty line. In terms of availability of basic facilities in her house, there is no much difference between her family and the families of other panchayat representatives because she also lives in the *kaccha* house, which is electrified but handpump, toilet, and separate drawing room facility is not available. Also, there is lack of modern household assets but the family has television, radio and cooler facility.

Like her father/husband she is also active member of Congress Party since even before 1990, but as yet she has not actively participated in *Dharna* or rally etc. She is also not associated with any social organisation. Her father-in-law is influential person in the area.

The family owns about 8 acres of irrigated land. The only source of irrigation is privately owned well. The family took loan of more than Rs. 5000 for well and brick kiln construction. Also, it has saving of more than Rs. 5000 only.

She contested the 1994 election for the post of sarpanch unsuccessfully. She was defeated because two persons of the same village had contested for Sarpanch post. But she won the 1999 election by the margin of 6 votes. As yet she has attended training programme upto seven days at Jabalpur, Hyderabad and Delhi. During the training programme she learnt about the rural development schemes as well as rights and duties of PR representatives. To her such programme should be launched on constant basis. Whatever she learnt in the training she passed on it to the villagers and also she discussed it with the officials.

The level of her awareness is relatively higher. She knows that the new PR was introduced during 1994 in order to reintroduce development schemes in a proper way. Since she frequently moves in the area, therefore she knows that the problem of road, school building and drinking water are the serious issues in her locality. She is satisfied with the rights extended to the J.P. President but these rights are not actualized due to shortage of fund. However, because of her experience in panchayat as a panch in the past, she knows how to deal with the local problems. She won the election by constant convasing. The family members, particularly the father-in-law who is influential and the villagers helped her to win both the elections in the panchayat. She is satisfied with the work like construction of bridge on the local river, school building, house for the poor etc. and she is confident that in the next election also people will help her to win it because of her performance. She is hopeful that in the remaining part of her tenure she will do all the incomplete/new work as desired by the villagers. For this she will organise and motivate panches/sarpanches to cooperate her. She opined that had there been non-tribal representative at her place he/she may not have done work for tribal development. She said that due to non-assertiveness on the part of Panchayat representatives, people at large do not attend the *Gram Sabha's* meetings.

Ammu Singh

Ammu Singh represents relatively well to do tribal representative of Betul. This is because in comparison to his counterpart he lives in semi-*paccka* house, which is electrified along with telephone connection. He is Gond, about 50 years old, educated upto higher secondary level and engaged in farming work. Economic condition of the family is also better. In spite of the fact that he owns about 30 acres of cultivable land of which 23 acres is unirrigated. Ammu Singh is a member of Congress Party since long like his father, but he has neither participated in procession etc., nor he is associated with any social organisation. The family has some of modern agricultural and household assets like pumpset, tractor, fan and cooler etc.

Singh successfully contested the 1994-panchayat election for the same post and won the seat by the margin of 1 vote, but in the election of 1999 he defeated the nearest rival by 189 votes. He feels that he was voted because of his excellent performance in the previous tenure. Singh participated in a training programme which was conducted for two days. He learnt about his rights and duties, fund and its use and other things. Therefore, he feels that such training programmes should regularly be organised.

Although this is his second term in panchayat, but he neither knows the year when new panchayat system was introduced nor he knows objectives behind its introduction. However, villagers have some hope from him. They want road, drainage facility, regular water supply from the local tank and high school facility. But he said that he is unable to fulfil such desires because of shortage of appropriate amount of fund. It is true that in spite of unavailability of proper amount of fund under his leadership, local road and school building was constructed and some households were also provided handpump facility. He thinks that he will contest the next election for the same post in order to complete the incomplete work. He is confident that looking to his past performance, the villagers will help him to win the election. Although, he is a member of Congress Party but because of his rapport with BJP workers, he is smoothly running the panchayat since iast two tenures. He has successfully constructed several buildings. Therefore, he considers himself more superior in comparison to other panchayat representatives. Also, he feels that his panchayat is more developed than other panchayats. He said that if the limit of current fund is increased, if he is again elected as sarpanch and if co-workers extend their support honestly, surely he can do something for the cause of his panchayat. He also feels that had there been non-tribal representative at his place, it would have been impossible for him to work like him. So far as generation of fund at the local level is concerned, it is very difficult task for him, but he is successful in managing various disputes at his level. Further, participation of local women in panchayat activities is yet to get momentum under his leadership.

On the basis of analysis of five cases it can be said that tribal leadership in gram panchayat is in the hands of both rich and the poor people. They have links with the political parties. At the performance level those who have links with more than one political parties they are doing well. Whatever they do it is totally dependent on the government grant. Poverty-ridden situation do not allow them to generate revenue from the villagers. The level of awareness have increased over the time. The role of training programme is significant in this matter.

5

Conclusion

Panchayat Raj institution (PRI) was introduced in order to ensure participation of cross-section of people living at the grassroots in the management of development process for overall improvement in the physical and social quality of life of the common people. In spite of apprehension from different corners that it will work in favour of the dominants only. (Ambedkar, reprint 1995). The thinking of the dominant social and political order was that this experiment will contribute to devolution of power upto the micro level resulting thereby people's participation across their background in the regulation of development programmes as per their own choice, culture, custom and traditions. But when we look into the scenario after fifty years of its introduction the apprehension became reality. The marginalized and their concerns remained far away from the scope of PRI in the real sense. Some of the broad factors contributing to near stagnation of PRI were: lack of proper understanding of the scope and methodology of integrated, multi-level decentralizing planning at different levels and tasks needed to be performed, restrictions imposed by the government on panchayats in the performance of their functions, existence of parallel bodies to perform the same functions, lack of technical knowledge and dearth of suitable personal, inadequate financial resources, politicization of the system, unwillingness to grant authority and power institutions at different levels by politicians and bureaucracy. Further, studies conducted in Gujarat and Karnataka observed that panchayat served the interest of mainly one group, namely the group of big farmers and rich traders usually belonging to the higher castes. The SC/ST members of panchayat were co-opted by the elite group and they really did not represent the interests of the poor in the panchayats and therefore, the masses and the poor had practically no say in the decision-making process in the panchayat, with the result that the activities of the panchayat did not serve the interests of the poor in development activities.

Hence, critically speaking in principle, the ideals of PRI was based on the spirit of self-reliance, self-help and self-imitation, but in practice different picture emerged. It did not contribute to the formation of effective leadership among cross-sections of villagers. The leadership remained in the hands of upper segments of society. It worked for the rich. The masses of the poor did not gain much out of the system, rather they were exploited by the PRI leaders.

73rd Constitutional Amendment and the Weaker Sections

In order to provide new face to the PRI so that it may practically come closer to the marginalised, the 73rd Constitutional amendment was passed. This amendment is in operation since 1994. There are different features of this amendment. However, from the point of view of empowerment of weaker sections it is for the first time that reservation of seats for SC/ST have been provided for in proportion to their population size at all the three levels of the PRI. Till date only few of them were seen in the PRI and that too not in an assertive and interactive position. Most of them were the coopted members and therefore their behaviour was proxy in nature. The 73rd Constitutional amendment empowered them to contest election safely on the reserved seats. Critically speaking by making and implementing such provision it is for the first time that the state really made effort to respect Article 46 of the Indian Constitution and protect and promote economic and educational interests of the weaker sections. Because of enforcement of this provision today there are 52726 and 90861 Panchayat representatives in Madhya Pradesh from the SC and ST respectively.

Beside the reservation facility, which led to joining of thousands of dalits and tribals in the PRI, various efforts like training programme, provision of no confidence motion on objective basis, NGO intervention etc. have been made for their empowerment. Also, during last few years many provisions have been made to safeguard these representatives from any type of encroachment. Because of these interventions one can expect emergence of effective and responsive leadership from among the marginalized.

But it is needless to mention that socio-economic environment in most of the villages in M.P. are still not in favour of the marginalized. In fact there is a conflict between emerging democratic values and the established particularistic socio-cultural values in most of the villages. Under the given situation how and to what extent the dalit and tribal leaders in the PRI feel effective and empowered and to what extent they are successful in institutionalizing democratic values is a matter which needs to be probed.

Objectives

The specific objectives of this study are the following :

- to know background of the dalit/tribal leaders in order to examine whether there is similarities between them and the masses in terms of their social status;
- to examine main concerns of the dalit/tribal masses as perceived by the Dalit/Tribal PRI leaders, community members and others;
- to discuss the amount of involvement/non-involvement of these leaders in the solution of the problems of common dalit/tribal masses;
- to explore facilitating/inhibiting factors in the effective functioning or non-functioning of the leadership; and
- to suggest mechanisms to ensure effective interplay between the PRI and the marginalized.

Universe

In order to search answer of these issues study was conducted in the Sehore Block of Sehore district and Betul Block of Betul district of Madhya Pradesh. In Madhya Pradesh SC and ST constitute about 16 and 20 per cent of population respectively. In

Betul Block ST constitutes about 38 per cent and in Sehore Development Block SC constitutes about 20 per cent of population. *Dobhi*, *Nai* and *Chamar* constitute the major population of Scheduled Castes in Sehore while *Gond* and *Korku* are the major tribes in Betul block. From the point of view of per capita income, landholding, literacy, availability of health facilities and infrastructure etc., the area in general and ST and SC population in particular are underdeveloped. In other words, both the area and its population are by and large underdeveloped. The main source of livelihood in both the districts are agriculture.

Sampling

There are 77 gram panchayats in Betul Block. The study was conduced in 50 gram panchayats. However, from within 50 Panchayats only those Panchayat Representatives were selected for study who are tribals. Altogether 250 Panchayat representatives participated in the study. Their position in the PRI was like this: Sarpanch 24, Panch 217, J.P. President 1, J.P. Member 7 and Z.P. Member 1. There are 127 gram panchayats in Sehore block, 24 are headed by the Dalit Sarpanches, i.e. 16 men and 8 women. We could interview only 6 Sarpanches. But 20 dalit panches and 1 J.P. member and 1 Z.P. member were also interviewed. Hence, 28 dalit representatives participated in the study.

Instrument

Semi-structured interview schedule was the main instrument of data collection. It was administered on the Panchayat representatives. But interview guide was administered on community members, and local level government officials dealing with PRI. Perception of "others" helped to make comparative analysis of the views expressed by the panchayat representatives on different aspects of panchayat and the marginalized interface.

Findings and Discussion

Profile of the respondents

Majority of the tribal respondents in Betul are between the age group of 25 to 44 years, married, either illiterate or just literate, engaged in agricultural activities and majority of them (63%) are from below the poverty line.

In the case of Sehore also majority of the Dalit respondents are between the age group of 25 to 44 years, they are married, illiterate or just literate, engaged in agricultural activities and wage work and most of them (82%) are from below the poverty line.

Political affiliation

Today it is the Congress Party which rules the state since last nine years. In the case of Betul about 66 per cent of the respondents (out of 250) are the members of political parties. 14.8, 28.4 and 26 per cent respondents are the members of political parties before 1990, between 1990 and 1995 and since 1995 respectively. However, 165 are the members of Congress Party. But except taking part in voting very few of them take part in other political activities.

In the case of Sehore out of 28 dalit respondents 12 are the members of political parties. Ten of them are the members since 1990. Eight are the members of Congress Party and the remaining 4 are of BJP Here also none of them take part in any political activities except casting their votes. (Chaudhary, 2002)

On the basis of above analysis it is clear that the social and economic background of the dalit and tribal leaders in both the districts is almost similar to the dalit and tribal population living in these two districts. In Sehore and Betul districts 81 and 85 per cent population is engaged in agricultural activities respectively. Under the given situation the Panchayat leaders are supposed to truthfully represent the masses. It is also assumed that since most of the PRI leaders are associated with Congress Party, the party which is in power, therefore these leaders are supposed to receive proper and sufficient resources from the state.

Perception about local issues

Since there is no caste/community and class distinction between the panchayat representatives and the villagers, since the representatives live with the people, since they themselves witness village level problems and issues therefore, it is assumed that both the representatives and the community members will have similar opinions about the main concerns of the people and the area as well as it is also assumed that the level of performance by these representatives must be high.

It is observed that in spite of social and cultural similarity between the villagers and the Panchayat representatives both of them have (i) different perceptions about the local level problems and therefore (ii) the money spent by the panchayats are as per the guidelines of the government or the panchayat representatives and not as per the preferences of the people.

On the basis of above perceptions it is clear that broadly there is difference between the views of community members and the government officials regarding the major problems in the villages. While drinking water is the most serious problem as per the perception of community members in Betul, the government officials perceive lack of road as the serious problem. The perception of panchayat representatives stands in between the two extremes. Ninety-one respondents (all panches) do not see any serious problem in the village and for 76 underdevelopment of the village is the serious problem. Further, 50 perceive lack of employment opportunity as the serious problem. It is needless to mention that lack of school, health and drinking water facility is perceived as a serious problem only by 4, 1 and 13 respondents respectively. On this basis it is clear that non-economic (social) issues are the serious problem for the villagers and economic/infrastructural backwardness is the serious problem for the panchayat representatives and the government officials.

In the case of Sehore also lack of employment opportunity, high migration, high indebtedness, high landlessness, lack of drinking water etc. is perceived as the serious problem by the panchayat representatives. The problem of education is seriously perceived by only a single respondent. Out of 28 dalit respondents nobody perceived untouchability, lack of health facility as a serious problem. Otherwise, it is needless to mention that untouchability and alcoholism is the most serious dalit specific problem in Sehore.

Achievement of Tribal/Dalit leaders

About 40 per cent respondents from Betul have not done any concrete work in their panchayats. All of them are panches. Fourty-five respondents constructed village road, provided handpumps, tank and school building in the villages. Some respondents constructed more than one structure of different type. Eleven per cent constructed village road, drainage system, handpump, village bridge, panchayat building, water tank, village *choupal* etc. However, work for the development of people from health, education and women's empowerment point of view was done by not even a couple of respondents. This shows that for the representatives, development refers to merely construction work and it did not include social, economic and cultural aspects of life under the umbrella of development. It is possible that they might have done some work in this area, but they do not consider such work under the purview of development.

In the case of Sehore also more or less similar type of work was done by the dalit representatives. Some of the major works done by them are : road construction, house construction under IAY, handpump facility, preparation of proposal, management of land related papers, bridge construction etc. Unfortunately speaking none of these works are exclusively or only related to the development of dalits. Two very serious dalit specific problems prevalent in Sehore area are untouchability and alcoholism. Practice of these two problems have negatively affected dignified life and therefore human rights of dalits. But these two problems have not been addressed by any of our 28 dalit respondents.

Why it is so that the Dalit and the Tribal representatives do not address the social issues? Some of the reasons are the following: (i) they receive prioritized budget. Most of these amounts are related to infrastructural development. Representatives have just to follow the guideline, (ii) it is easy to show construction work to the voters. In response to the question that what they have done during the last four years most of the representatives narrated the construction work, and (iii) in the case of construction work it is easy to oblige "others" and get them in confidence which help the representatives to run the panchayat in the smooth manner.

Difficulties

Significant number of dalit and tribal representatives have for the first time joined the PRI. They are from the lower social and economic status. Their exposure to outside world and level of awareness is very low. Given the situation many of them have to face difficulties in their day to day activities. And those who attempt to do something have to face more problems.

In the case of Betul about 50 per cent respondents, mostly panches, have to face more than one problem in the day-to-day activities. For example, 19 per cent perceive shortage/lack of grants as the main source of difficulty. Similar number of them accuse poor state of affair in the field of basic amenities as the source of difficulty. For 8 panches, sarpanch is the problem creator. Pappu (panch) said that with the help of the villagers he prepares proposal. It is submitted to Sarpanch for necessary action. But instead of forwarding it to the higher officials he sats on it. He kills spirit. Today people at large do not attend the *Gram Sabha* meeting as they used to attend few years ago. This is because they do not find it beneficial. It is needless to mention that soon after the first panchayat election in1994 government constructed *pucca* Panchayat Bhavan. In many of the *Bhavans* television sets were also installed. Seeing this development the villagers perceived Panchayat as a rich organization to deal with their economic problem. Hence, large number of villagers attended *Gram Sabha* meeting those days. But in the due course after attending several meetings they did not receive anything. As a result their interest was killed. This feeling has negatively contributed to people's participation in Panchayat activities. Under the given circumstances Panchayat representatives do not get support of the largely attended *gram sabha*, and approval of proposal by *Gram Sabha* becomes a routinised affair. Fifty-one Panches said that they are not heard by anybody, they have personal loss particularly wage loss after joining PRI, they are also criticized by the villagers for their non-performance. One of the respondent (Panch) said that he was engaged in the construction of village road. All of a sudden Sarpanch and the panchayat Secretary were engaged by the government. in the *Gram Smapark Abhiyan.* It consumed all the money, hence, the construction work was discontinued. Mani Ram (J.P. Member) of Hathanjiri panchayat said, "I placed a demand of tank, road, telephone and bridge in my panchayat but at the J.P. level Panchayat representatives did not care for my demand. They do not approve any of my demand because I am not powerful." But Dullo Bai (Panch) of Malkapur accused the sarpanch for his non-performance. She said, "sarpanch works under the pressure of influentials of Malkapur village. Actually somebody else from my village was elected as Sarpanch. But at the time of counting electricity was off. The present Sarpanch managed the ballot and was declared elected. We did not do anything. Today the Sarpanch is failed to seek support of the villagers."

Twenty-eight dalit representatives from Sehore participated in the study. 10 do not face any difficulty. This is because they are Panches and most of them (8) have done nothing as yet. They perceive themselves simply as signature master. The others have to face problems. For example, 3 said that since they are from the lower class therefore nobody listens to them. Similar number of them said that since the Sarpanch is non-dalit, therefore they seldom listen to them. One of the respondents said that whatever proposal is submitted by him it is rejected. A Dalit Panch of Lasuria Panchayat, Jai Singh said, "Since Dalits are in less number in Panchayat body, therefore, non-dalit members, who are in large number, do not listen to them. We most often oppose their unacceptable views in the meeting unsuccessfully. People from general category dominate in our Panchayat. We as a dalit representatives are failed to avail any benefit from the panchayat body." One of the dalit women Sarpanch narrated her plight that the then Sarpanch had misused the fund. Hence, government think that she will also misuse the fund. Therefore, they are not releasing the fund. In order to overcome this problem, she published her plight in the local newspaper and also wrote an application to the higher authorities but nothing came out. One dalit Panch said that he is not heard because he is illiterate. He said that only those dalits are active and assertive who are powerful. Hem Raj Jatav (SC) Panch of Barahgarh Panchayat said, "Sarpanch and others only sent papers to me for signature, they never inform me to attend any meeting." It is needless to mention that Jatav is a marginal farmer and his family is under debt since long.

In order to overcome the above problem many of the dalits (15) do not take any step. Two of them even do not hesitate to provide bribe to get their work done. But none of these representatives organise themselves, discuss and formulate strategies to overcome problems created by the local and block level functionaries. Rather in most of the cases they expect help from "others".

Ensuring Strong Interface between PRI and the Marginalized

Under the given circumstances when PRI representatives lack social capital, face problems from different cornors at the local level and do not make distinction between construction and development and for construction work they are totally dependent on state and therefore face state centred problems like corruption, bureaucratic delay, prioritization of schemes and allotment of fund accordingly and so on, it is very difficult to ensure effective functioning of Panchayats. This state of affair is contributed by lack of capacity and will on the part of the representatives to impose tax on the villagers because it will displease the supporters. Majority of the representatives do not cover social agenda in their manifesto because fund is relatively limited, investment in social sector is long term in nature and it is different to quantify and demonstrate the achievement. Under the given situation how the main concern of the villagers including the social aspect of development will become concern of panchyats? Respondents from both Betul and Sehore perceive this question in the following manner.

In Betul none of the respondents consider social development as part of development. To them construction refers to development. 126 didn't make any comment. The remaining 124 suggested strategies to ensure effective functioning of panchyat primarily in the economic sense. They said that by ensuring cooperation from the government officials, organizing training on regular basis, putting check on personal likings and dislikings of Sarpanch, encouraging larger participation in *Gram Sabha* meeting (and this is possible provided people's problem are addressed quickly), increasing fund and its release in time, fixing accountability on panchayat secretary etc., the functioning of PRI may be strengthened. More or less similar suggestions were made by the *Garm Sabha* members and the government officials. But none of the respondents answered the question that how the Panchayat will function if government grant is not made available?

In Sehore also none of the respondents made suggestion to include dimensions of social development under the umbrella of construction based development. In response to the question that how problem of dalits may be successfully addressed by the dalit headed Panchayats, 36 per cent respondents said that their demands/problems should first of all be heard honestly by those who are in the healms of affair. It was also suggested that by motivating non-dalit Sarpanch and J.P. representatives, preparing BPL list honestly, awaring dalits in general and dalit representatives in particular, providing land to the landless dalits, creating employment opportunities at the local level and organizing training programme on constant basis, dalit headed Panchayats may be made effective. Batanlal, a dalit Panch of Bichia Panchayat suggested:

> "General Caste people do not allow us to speak. If I will speak I will invite trouble for me. Nobody listen to me in *gram sabha* and Panchayat meeting because I am dalit. Government should again and again say the non-dalits to listen to our voice."

A significant number of respondents said that without empowering dalit masses particularly in economic terms, one cannot empower dalit leaders and address the problems of dalits. If the dalit masses are mouthless and voiceless how can their leaders may become powerful asked one of the dalit leaders. Dwarka Singh, a dalit Panch of Thuna Kala Panchayat suggested:

"Near the forest area about 800 acres of land are lying vacant. All the landless dalits of my panchayat should be allotted upto 2.5 acres of land out of this lying land. This will reduce their economic dependence resulting thereby empowerment of the dalit masses."

On the basis of above discussion it is clear that today due to reservation facility under the 73rd Constitutional amendment there are thousands of Dalit and Tribal leaders in panchayats at all the three levels. Some of them have done wonderful work. But many of them are the first generation entrant in politics, they are from lower socio-economic status and they are notionally capacitated to understand their rights and duties. Therefore,. at the decision and action level many of them are dependent on others including the Panchayat Secretary. As a result they are manipulated by others. They have done some work but most of these works are related to infrastructural development. These works cannot be sustainable because it has been done only due to government support. Representatives are failed to generate resources at the local level partly because they think that villagers are not capable to give tax and partly due to fear of disintegration of their support base. Under this situation if the government grant is discontinued they cannot continue construction work. And to seek government grant they have to follow all the means as followed by others. They blindly follow the schemes imposed by the government. This is because fund is easily available for the work already prioritized by the government. In case they formulate their own scheme and send it to J.P. Panchayat or higher level office after the approval of the *Gram Sabha* in many of the cases it is seldom approved. In case it is approved it takes lot of time to actualize the project. Reservation has given them position. But success of *gram sabha*, constant training programme, effective implementation of anti-poverty schemes and NGO intervention can only empower them. Today the nature of support from *gram sabha* is not strong at all. People at large are not enthusiastic to attend the meeting. Training has sharp but limited impact. Similar is the situation with the NGO intervention. In such a situation in order to empower dalit and tribal leadership and making the agenda of this segment such as untouchability in Sehore and lack of drinking water in Betul. In the main agenda of Panchayat it is essential that the *gram sabha* is strengthened, common cause is addressed honestly, training programme for *gram sabha* members, Panchayat representatives and secretaries are organised on regular basis, government is pressed to release grant in time, achievement of Panchayat is publicly demonstrated among the villagers, then only we can see the effective functioning of democracy at the village level under the emerging dalit and tribal leadership.

Bibliography

Ali, Saliq (1964): *Report of the Study Team on Panchayati Raj*, Jaipur: Panchayat and Development, Govt. of Rajasthan.

Adiseshaiah (1964): *Social background and role preference of village Pradhans*, New Delhi: Institute of Social Sciences, p.39.

Aziz, A. (2000): "Democratic, Decentralization – Experience of Karnataka", *Economic and Political Weekly*, Vol. XXXV, No. 39, Sept. 23-29.

Ambedkar, B.R. (1995): *Writings and Speeches*, Vol. 13, Education Deptt., Govt. of Maharashtra, p.62.

Buch, N., Jain, U. and Chaudhary, S.N. (1999): *Women in Panchayati Raj in Madhya Pradesh*, (Mimeo) Bhopal: Mahila Chetna Manch.

B.R. Mehta Committee Report (1957): *Report of the Team for the Study of Community Projects and National Extension Service*, New Delhi.

Chaudhary, S.N. (2002): *Dalit Leadership in Panchayats: The Case of Madhya Pradesh*, (Mimeo) PRIA, New Delhi.

Chaudhary, S.N. (2003): *Emerging patterns of Tribal leadership in Gram Panchayat: A study of their social background, level of awareness and aspirations*, (unpublished) Report submitted to MAPCOST, Bhopal.

Datta, Bishaka (ed.), (1997): "The amount of work the ladies did, the men will not do and who will make the chapatis: A study of All-Women Panchayats in Maharashtra", Calcutta; Stree.

Gurumurthy, U. (1987): *Panchayati Raj and the Weaker Section*, New Delhi: Ashish Publishing House, p.168.

Govt. of Madhya Pradesh (1998): *The Madhya Pradesh Human Development Report*, Bhopal.

Hirway, I. (1986): "Panchayat-Raj at Crossroads", *Economic and Political Weekly*, July 22, pp. 1663-1667.

Kanango, S.D. (1996): "Panchayati-Raj and Emerging Women Leadership: An Overview", *Social Action*, Vol. 46, January-March.

Lele, M.K. (2001): "Local Government: Conflict of Interests and Issues of Legitimization", *Economic and Political Weekly*, Vol. XXXVI, No. 51, Dec. 22-28.

Murthy, O.K. (1969): *Some Reflections on the duplication of Panchayati-Raj on the Weaker Sections of the Community*, in the proceedings of the 15th Conference of the K.S. Co.

Mahipal (1998): "Women in Panchayat: Experiences of a Training Camp", *Economic and Political Weekly*, Vol. XXIII, No.4, Jan.24-30, pp. 150-152.

Nayak, R.C. and George Mathew (1996): "Panchayat at work: What it means for the oppressed?," *Economic and Political Weekly*, July 6, p.20.

Parvathamma (1975): "Panchayati-Raj and Weaker Sections", presented at the seminar held in NIRD, Hyderabad (Unpublished paper).

Pai, S. (1998): "Pradhanis in New Panchayats : Fields notes from Meerut district", *Economic and Political Weekly*, Vol. XXIII, No. 18, May 2-8, pp. 1009-10.

Pai, S. (2001): "Social Capital, Panchayat and Grassroots Democracy: Politics of Dalit Assertion in Uttar Pradesh", *Economic and Political Weekly*, Vol. XXXVI, No. 8, Feb. 24-Mar. 2.

Pundir, J.K. (1995): "Development of Scheduled Castes: A Study of their Political and Decisive Participation at local level in rural areas", *AJSDJ*, Vol. III, pp.49-64.

Randhawa, N.S. (1996): "Panchayati Raj System for Decentralized Planning – Myths and Realities", *Man and Development*, 1996.

Shyamala, C.K. (2001): "Elected Representation in Rural Decentralized Governance: Socio-economic analysis of Zilla Panchayat Members in Karnataka", *Man and Development*, June.

Sheshadri, B. and Azim, S. (2001): "Evaluation of Decentralized Governance and Planning in Karnataka", *Man and Development*, June.

Singh, D.R. (1985): *Rural Leadership among Scheduled Castes*, Allahabad: Chugh Publications, pp.189-202.

Singh, A.K. (1996): "Panchayati-Raj Legislation in selected states – A comparative study", *Man and Development*, Sep.

Shiviah, M. (1976): *Panchayati-Raj : An Analytical Survey*, Hyderabad: NIRD.

INDEX